D0408254

THE COMPLETE GUIDE TO

Buying and Selling
at Auction

THE COMPLETE GUIDE TO
Buying and Selling at Auction

C. Hugh Hildesley

A GINIGER BOOK *published in association with*
W·W·NORTON & COMPANY· *NEW YORK· LONDON*

*This book is composed in Palatino. Composition and manufacturing are by the
Maple-Vail Book Manufacturing Group. Book design is by Marjorie J. Flock.*

Library of Congress Cataloging-in-Publication Data

Hildesley, C. Hugh.
    The complete guide to buying and selling at auction / C. Hugh
Hildesley.
      p.   cm.
    Includes index.
    ISBN 0-393-04071-2
    1. Auctions.   I. Hildesley, C. Hugh. Sotheby's guide to buying
and selling at auction. II. Title.
HF5476.H49   1997
658.8′4—dc21   96-39263
                                                 CIP

Published in association with the K. S. Giniger Company, Inc.,
235 Park Avenue South, New York, NY 10003.

W. W. Norton & Company, Inc., 500 Fifth Avenue, New York, N.Y. 10110
http://www.wwnorton.com

W. W. Norton & Company Ltd., 10 Coptic Street, London WC1A 1PU

2 3 4 5 6 7 8 9 0

To my colleagues at Sotheby's, in gratitude

Contents

Sample Documents and Catalogue Pages

Introduction

AUCTION, the method of selling by which property passes from the seller to the buyer at the highest price offered in a public forum, must be almost as old a method of trading as civilization itself. It would not be stretching the imagination very far to envisage the prehistoric hunter, dragging his dead woolly mammoth into the middle of the clearing in front of the caves, summoning his fellow hunter-gatherers, and offering choice portions of his trophy to his eager fellow providers.

"What am I offered for this choice section of the flank? Do I hear one cowrie shell . . . ?"

It is known that in ancient Babylon, auction was the method of choice in the white slave trade, and, indeed, slave auctions continued in America into the nineteenth century. The first auctions in America were conducted by foreign merchants, whose activities were sufficiently similar to later practitioners at Atlantic City that they were restricted by law to conducting their sales "by public outcry" below the high-water mark on the beaches.

Fine-arts auctions as we know them began in earnest in the eighteenth century in England, although it should be remembered that Rembrandt's own art collection was disposed of at auction in Amsterdam in December 1657 to satisfy his ever-increasing debts. On the sixteenth of May in 1697, 21 works by an artist whose premature death left the world with a scant 36 masterpieces, Jan Vermeer of

Delft, were sold, providing one of the earliest examples of a studio sale. The principal buyer was Jacob Abrahamsz. Dissius of Delft, who owned 19 of the artist's works at the end of the seventeenth century.

But it was in the middle of the eighteenth century that the two principal fine-arts auctioneers in London made their appearance, responding to the huge increase in collecting and the flourishing of the great country homes and libraries that became the mark of civilization of the newly wealthy English gentry. It only took one generation of collecting for heirs to recognize the choice they could make between keeping a collection intact or selling it to provide cash for alternative uses.

While Messrs. Sotheby, Wilkinson, and Hodge might have difficulty in recognizing their profession in a major impressionist night sale today, with twenty or more international telephone links, a sales clerk feeding a computer beside the auctioneer, an electronic currency converter exhibiting the bids in five or six currencies simultaneously, closed-circuit television links to subsidiary salesrooms, and a rash of cellular phones keeping agent and client in perpetual contact, they would, nevertheless, see at the center of the action an auctioneer in a familiar-looking rostrum, taking bids in an orderly, time-honored sequence, and completing the transaction by banging down his or her ivory hammer or gavel. At least that part of the ritual remains unchanged since Thomas Rowlandson's depiction of an eighteenth-century book auction at Sotheby's (see Figure 1). Auction remains a highly effective method for the buying and selling of all kinds of works of art. The magic of the auction room continues to play its part. The salesroom remains the best place to determine the fair market value of a work of art, providing the best barometer of supply and demand within every field of collecting.

It was, indeed, books, manuscripts, and printed materials that preoccupied Sotheby's until the end of the nineteenth century. Christie's, who entered the field twenty-two years after Sotheby's, sold paintings and decorative arts from its inception, maintaining a closer social tie with the great families of England and spawning a long-lasting but now inaccurate distinction between the two firms, summarized by the statement that "Sotheby's was a group of dealers pretending to be gentlemen, and Christie's was a group of gentlemen pretending to be dealers."

Figure 1. Thomas Rowlandson, *Sotheby's*

It is not, however, the purpose of this book to write the history of auction sales nor even the history of a particular auction room, but, rather, to take you, the reader, on a journey through the entire auction process, from first contact to final settlement, demystifying that process and, at the same time, encouraging you to use the resources made available to the public by the auction room. You will also be made aware of the full services offered to the collector by the auction house, which provides so much more than the sales transaction itself. The auction house is in some ways like a museum whose stock changes once a week, but a museum with three major distinctions. You are encouraged to touch the items on display; everything in the exhibition is available for sale to you; and items of differing quality are shown together, enabling you to acquire a knowledge, through detailed inspection and comparison, of what constitutes the best quality in a given area. As with the museum, a large group of specialists are available to share their expertise with you at no charge and with no compulsion to buy or sell.

Thus, whether you intend to sell, buy, or just browse, this book is offered as a practical introductory guide for the uninitiated, who, it is hoped, will as a result become acquainted with the fascination and pleasure derived from participating in the auction world.

THE COMPLETE GUIDE TO

Buying and Selling at Auction

I

Inside the Auction House

Who Works at an Auction House?

Given the heavy volume of business—167,000 lots, many of them comprising multiple objects, passed through Sotheby's worldwide in 1995—it will not be surprising that an auction operation is extremely labor-intensive. The average item moves at least fifteen times between arrival and final delivery. Expertly trained staff are on hand to make these moves safe and effective. For every work of art there is a specialist who will be involved in receipting, researching, describing, and then promoting it as accurately as possible against a demanding catalogue deadline. Each item must be photographed, in itself a complicated and highly skilled task. The publication of the sales catalogue, which reflects the research and scholarship involved in presenting a work of art at auction, demands the same attention to detail and professionalism that is to be found in the finest art publishing houses. The accuracy of a catalogue remains an essential element in the process of presenting a work of art in the salesroom. The reputation of the house rests on such accuracy. Supporting the expert departments, along with the Photography Department, are the Catalogue Production Department, which produces one catalogue a day at the height of the season; the Marketing Division, which is responsible for the worldwide advertising and promotion of the sales; and a Press Department, which is responsible for seeing that the public is constantly aware of the activities of the auction house, not only in achieving world records for the dramatic masterpieces by Picasso, but also in attracting the regular customer, who can take advantage of the fact that some 80 percent of the items sold at auction in a given year fetch under $5,000, a fact that should encourage the neophyte to jump into the world of collecting.

Behind every transaction—and it must be remembered that in a regular auction sale, we may be selling as many as 2 lots per minute—there lies a huge financial and accounting operation, not to mention a Legal Department, making sure that we are selling the property according to a previously agreed-upon contract. The Client Services Division is available to bid on behalf of absent clients, who on occasion may be linked to them by live telephone connection in the salesroom; to offer condition reports and pass on the advice of the experts on a particular lot; not to mention to organize shipment, restoration or repair, and the sending of transparencies to potential buyers. In effect, the auction house combines the functions of a museum, a publishing house, a department store, a theater, and even a restaurant.

The most important persons who work at an auction room are, however, the specialists, without whom there would be no business. Let us, then, take a look at these remarkable people. Where do they come from? How are they trained? What do they do on a daily basis? My own story is not atypical and may prove instructive.

At the age of nineteen, having completed one year at Oxford University, a period in which it became evident that I was never going to succeed as a lawyer, I was faced with the challenge of finding something to do. Having studied art history at school, I knew the arts intrigued me but was willing to admit that my knowledge was scanty at best. A family friend who worked with a prominent

London art gallery graciously consented to interview me and gently explained that, since I knew nothing about art, I would be of little use to his renowned gallery. But might I consider working at one of the auction galleries, where I would gain some experience of how the art market worked and, thus, prove more employable after a period of years? His first introduction led me to Christie's, where a young expert in the Old Master Department took me out to coffee in Jermyn Street and explained that in 1961 there were already far too many young men in the art market. Undaunted by this wisdom from a twenty-three year old, I immediately followed up on my second introduction to a young director of British paintings at Sotheby's.

On the hottest day of August in 1961—it must have been at least 80 degrees—I was ushered into a small office in the basement of 34 New Bond Street. There sat one of the then ten private partners who presided over the relatively small auction house, proud of the latest season's turnover of $28,834,100, just a little less than the price of the single Picasso from the Stralem Collection, sold on May 8, 1995, in New York for $29.2 million (see Figure 2) but a considerable improvement from the turnover for the founding year of 1744, in which the firm sold £826 sterling worth of books and literary material. My interviewer was impressively tall and appeared to be considerably over-weight. The sun beat down upon a skylight that covered the entire ceiling of his small office. Air conditioning was unheard of in London at this time, and the partner in question had clearly had a very good lunch. (I was to learn subsequently that his girth had to do with the fact that he had a very good lunch every day at a wonderful pub a few steps from Sotheby's—The Guinea, which still provides superb lunches.) The office was hotter than a sauna, and we both sat there in our thick English suits, sweating pro-fusely, I on account nervous anxiety, he on the basis of the heat and the physical manifestations of his recent prandial excess. At least he was under the impression that my perspiration was a sympathetic acknowledgment of the heat.

"What school did you go to?" was the opening salvo, as my interviewer mopped his brow with a silk handkerchief that gave off the scent of an expensive eau de cologne.

Figure 2. Pablo Picasso, *Angel Fernandez De Soto*

"Sherborne" I replied, recognizing that this fine old English public school was better known for its rugby football than for any artistic educational endeavors. Eton, Harrow, or Winchester would have been more popular responses since these three were the more traditional sources for young gentlemen of means.

"Not bad" was the partner's response, as if he might grant me a stay of execution, should I do better on the remaining questions—as it turned out, a forlorn hope. "Do you have any money?" was the next question, accompanied by further wiping of not only the brow but the entire neck.

Not sure if he was requesting an immediate small loan or inquiring as to whether I came from a family of means, I opted for the direct response: "No!"

"That's a pity because we don't pay our trainees very much. Which department were you planing to join?"

"Paintings, sir." At last I was on firmer ground, or so I thought.

"My dear young man, there are at least four painting departments. Which one did you have in mind?"

Having not thought specifically about this refinement, I was somewhat at a loss as to where to go with this question. My minimal introduction to art history had at least led me to the knowledge that there were old-master paintings and modern paintings, and I had heard of Rubens and Rembrandt but felt a little shakey in the impressionist and modern fields. My future career hung in the balance. I opted for tradition. "Old Masters?"

"Very well, report to the office manager at seven thirty on Monday morning. You will be an apprentice porter in the Old Master Painting Department, and you will receive four guineas, in cash, per week. Welcome to Sotheby's. That will be all. Good day!"

Pressing his limp, wet fleshy hand in mine, he conducted me to the door, mopping as he went. The entire interview had lasted less than five minutes. I bounded onto New Bond Street, scarcely able to believe my good fortune. I was an employee of Sotheby's. Miracles can and sometimes do happen.

The Specialist and the Work of Art

It is through its expert staffing that an auction house keeps available at all times experienced cataloguers, able to identify correctly any work of art brought in for inspection and evaluation. The correct presentation of an item for sale as described in the auction catalogue ensures the reputation of the auction house, whose clients rely on the breadth and depth of the expertise of the staff. These specialists must also know where to go for professional opinions when referrals are necessary or when an item falls outside the regular realm of business.

As the expert first examines a work of art, all sorts of questions are coursing through his or her mind. What is this? Where was it created? When was it created? How was it made? Who could have been responsible for its creation? Are there any distinguishing marks, a date, or a signature? What materials have been employed? When have I seen something similar? What did it make at sale? How would the market respond to this particular work? What condition is this work in? Has it been restored and, if so, how heavily? What should the sale estimate be for this work? What should the reserve or minimum be if we were to sell this work at auction? When is the next appropriate sale?

Not only must all the questions be answered, but the answers must be consistent in order for the identification to be satisfactory. With these questions in mind, let us take a look at an old-master painting, attributed to Jan van Goyen, to give an example of how the specialist thinks. The painting is *View of Dordrecht,* signed with the monogram "VG" and dated 1651 (see Figure 3).

What Is This?

A painting, or so it appears to be at first sight. But it may also be a reproduction, a painted-over photograph or print that has been mounted on canvas or panel and then varnished. It could be any number of types of fake, and the techniques have become extraordinarily sophisticated. Or is it a later copy of a well-known original or a painting in the style of a particular artist but painted at a later date?

Figure 3. Jan van Goyen, *View of Dordrecht*

Where Was It Created?

Narrowing down the geographical limits helps close the identification gap. Was our van Goyen painted on panel or canvas? It appears to be on panel, in which case we need to know what kind of wood we are dealing with. Should the painting be on a cypress panel, we have a problem. There are not too many cypress groves in Holland. Indeed, most Dutch painters of the seventeenth century painted on oak panels, the wood preferred by the guilds, who controlled the standards of artists' materials and often stamped the panels with their guild mark. Is the bevel of the panel consistent with the hand preparation of the panel, or is there evidence of a machine saw? Could this panel have been created in the seventeenth century? This is not to say that a genuine van Goyen painting could not have been transferred from its original panel to masonite during a twentieth-century restoration, but one should certainly seek documentary evidence if this appears to be the case. We know that van Goyen lived and worked in Dordrecht, and this view would have been familiar to him. There is no doubt that the church in the distance is the Grote Kerk, which dominates the horizon around Dordrecht to this day.

When Was It Created?

Assuming that we are, indeed, dealing with a Dutch panel, then the question of age arises. Various technical tests can be performed, although a specialist cannot move around the country with a full laboratory on wheels each time a painting is inspected. It is, thus, necessary to recognize some of the clues that a work of art gives as to its age. These clues will differ according to the work, but in the case of a Rembrandt, for instance, the expert will have studied the artist's technique, including his use of the brush and the methods by which he built up the paint layers, not to mention the fact that he often used the pointed end of his brush handle to incise the wet paint to achieve the effect of hair in his portraits. An artist's technique becomes as familiar to an expert as his or her own mother's handwriting. One recognizes the hand before "reading" the painting.

A further aid in detecting the age of a painting is the examination of the pattern of cracks that age creates on the painted surface. Neophytes sometimes express concern over these cracks. They should actually worry when the cracks are not present. If one thinks of a painting as containing several layers of material—panel or canvas, gesso, underpainting, several layers of paint, and several layers of varnish—it can be understood that over the years all these different materials respond to the climatic changes of temperature and humidity, responding to differing extents. The movements created by these changes send shock waves through the layers, producing prime, secondary, and tertiary cracking. This *craquelure* will assume distinguishable patterns on the basis of the materials involved and their age. It is possible, therefore, to tell the age of an old-master painting to within about twenty years on visual examination of these effects. Of course, it is a relatively easy matter to fake these effects—by baking the paint, incising the surface with a sharp point, rolling the canvas over an irregular stick, or even painting the *craquelure* onto the paint surface prior to applying one or more layers of yellowed varnish. Thus, it is necessary to determine that the *craquelure* has been the authentic result of the aging process.

Date may also be established by what I refer to as the *continuity test*. This requires a knowledge of the social history of a period. Are the costumes of the figures contemporary to the subject? Did that church exist in Dordrecht in 1650? Would the artist have been able to see a live dodo at such a date? (Yes, until the middle of the seventeenth century, by which time the Dutch sailors had eaten them all.) But, like the continuity experts in Hollywood, we need to be sure that Julius Caesar is not wearing a wrist watch, that there are no helicopters flying over the field of Agincourt, and that Rembrandt's sitter is not wearing a Calvin Klein undershirt or sitting next to a French eighteenth-century desk. Most paintings contain several reference points that can be subjected to this form of scrutiny. Our van Goyen is dated 1651. We must be sure that this inscription is authentic before relying on such information.

How Was It Made?

In the case of our van Goyen, this question has already been considered, but similar questions must be applied to every type of art. With furniture, for example, craftsmen from differing periods and locations will employ different materials and methods to join the various pieces of wood used in the construction of their products, and these methods will tend to be consistent within a period and a location. The comparison between English and American furniture of the last quarter of the eighteenth-century provides a useful illustration of this general assertion. The woods differ markedly, and the joining used in America shows Continental influences, indicating that colonial American craftsmen came from diverse backgrounds, which they were willing to combine to produce some of the finest furniture ever made. Thus, in every field the question of technique is an essential part of the identification process. How are bronzes cast? How is enamel created? How are ormolu mounts put together? What tools did the silversmith, engraver, and cabinetmaker use? What form did the nail take over the centuries? The history of clocks alone could occupy a lifetime.

Who Could Have Been Responsible for Its Creation?

The painting may have a date on it, but a date, like a signature, is surely one of the easiest things to add at a later opportunity. Although signatures and dates can be reassuring confirmation of a painting's authenticity, a true expert must reach a conclusion independent of such evidence.

The label on the frame of our painting says Jan van Goyen. A label on the reverse tells us that the painting was in the collection of the earl of Balfour. A letter has been passed down with the painting in which a nineteenth-century owner has bequeathed "My van Goyen painting to my niece Jane Doe," and the painting appears to be listed in C. Hofstede de Groot's catalogue raisonné. The landscape is signed with initials and dated "1651" in what appears to be the hand of the artist. And yet none of the above qualifies as conclusive evidence that our painting is by van Goyen. At best, the leading scholars of the day on this particular artist may reach a consensus as to the authorship of this particular work. Attribution cannot be totally objective. Unless one has by some miracle been able to be present with a work of art throughout its existence, one is left to rely upon the opinion of experts and the acceptance of the market itself, for, if the work is, indeed, by van Goyen, when it appears at auction appropriately described, it will reach a price commensurate with its historical importance. For an auction house's reputation to survive, it needs to be right as often as possible. It must be sufficiently confident of its specialists so that when they attribute a work of art to an artist, the vast majority of the world's experts will concur with that opinion.

Are There Any Distinguishing Marks—a Date or a Signature?

As has been stated, these marks are most easily reproduced; but a true expert can tell the difference between a true and false mark. Signatures can be compared in minute detail with existing genuine examples. Hallmarks on silver likewise can be placed next to known authentic impressions. Comparisons can be made to test the validity of dates. In every case, modern photography and other scientific devices can be brought to the task of determining the reliability of such information. The expert and the collector should maintain a healthy cynicism in this area since the work itself must, in the final analysis, be the test of authenticity. The reverse of the van Goyen has an inventory number from the Balfour Collection, an exhibition label from the 1962 show at the Dordrecht Museum, an auction-house number from the 1930s, and a wax seal from the Dutch family who owned the painting in the eighteenth century.

What Materials Have Been Employed?

With paintings, as with all other works of art, science can come to the aid of the art historian. Almost every material can be dated scientifically. It is not the purpose of this book to go into the details, but any art expert will readily guide the collector toward the technician who is capable of performing the relevant tests. Carbon 14 testing has done much to take the mystery out of the dating of ancient pottery and other three-dimensional objects. Sophisticated analysis is available in virtually every field. Competent and responsible restorers in any discipline can guide the collector toward such technical advice. In the case of major works of art, I see no reason to suggest that such testing is inappropriate. It is always useful to have one's personal intuition backed up by hard science. A dealer who is unwilling to subject a work of art to such scientific testing has presumably got something to hide. Connoisseurship should remain a combination of art and science. In the case of our van Goyen, the panel proves to be of oak, paint samples have tested out as seventeenth century, and the *craquelure* is appropriate to the date of the painting. A modern varnish has replaced the original, but there is no evidence of repaint or overpainting beneath this varnish.

When Have I Seen Something Similar?

A specialist's principal knowledge stems from experience in a particular field. My first experience was with Dutch seventeenth-century paintings. In the early years of my training, I was sent to The Hague to attend a course given by the Rijksbureau voor Kunsthistorische Documentatie, an institute for the study of Dutch art history attached to the University of The Hague. Here I spent an intense period of time being shown every work in every museum and major private collection, being tested at the end of each day by being shown slides and having to identify the artist, the subject, the date, and the museum location of any painting that was put on the screen. At the end of the period, I had amassed a vast file of Dutch paintings in my mind, against which I could measure any new painting that I encountered. Thus, when I visited a private collection and saw what purported to be an early river landscape by van Goyen, I could compare it mentally with the 1633 *View of Dordrecht* that I had seen in the museum in Rotterdam, not to mention the seven examples I had seen on exhibition at the Dordrecht Museum in the 1962 exhibition. In addition to this immensely valuable basic file, it must be remembered that at Sotheby's I might see as many as one hundred paintings a day of vastly differing quality and attribution. Specialists develop a photographic memory for the works of art in a particular field and think nothing of referring back to a painting or work of art that they saw once thirty years ago. I believe that this act of comparison, coupled with a detailed knowledge of market value and fluctuation, puts the auction-house expert at a great advantage in determining the current value of a work of art. The file of knowledge is vast, and the experience of the current market is central and second to none.

What Did It Make at Sale?

The specialist will usually have an accurate memory of recent sales. Should that memory prove elusive, the specialist has only to turn to the departmental records to know every price that has been achieved at auction in the past thirty years, and, thanks to computerization, worldwide auction prices in almost every field are available, either on-line or in published annual reports. There are stories, probably apocryphal, of collectors visiting African tribes in the hope of picking up some bargains in African masks, only to be greeted by the head of the tribe with the current volume of Sotheby's *Art at Auction* annual review in which the most recent prices are available. Sales prices are publicly available and can prove a useful guide to the collector; but, remember, it takes a real expert to interpret a list of prices since every work of art is unique, even though the subject, size, and date may appear to be identical, as we shall discover in a later section of this book. In the case of our van Goyen, I have prices as recent as last January's sale of old-master paintings in New York with which to make a comparison.

How Would the Market Respond to This Particular Work?

There is no question that the art market, as is true of any market, can be dramatically affected by prevailing conditions. The state of the economy and the activities of Wall Street are factors, but the art market seems also to run on its own set of principles. It must be remembered that the art market is not one market, but a series of markets, and that silver may be selling well while American furniture is flat. In part, this fluctuation has to do with the international nature of the markets and who is collecting what. Much has been made of the Japanese involvement in the impressionist and modern fields, and their departure, along with the tumble in our own financial market, caused major upsets in prices at the end of the 1980s. It is valid to ask the question "How is the art market as a whole?" and expect a competent observer of the auction market to give an answer. More relevant, however, is the question "How are old masters doing this season?" or "What happened to the sale of Russian icons last week in London?" Having established the state of the particular market, the question must still be asked: "How will this individual work of art fit into the auction market or potential sale?" Care must be taken not to flood the market with similar items. Some works of art are sufficiently unique that auction may not be the best method of disposal. Taste within a field changes, and collectors who are heavy play-ers in a certain field may only collect in one area of that given field. At one point, television producer Allen Funt collected only the works of the English nineteenth-cen-tury academician Sir Lawrence Alma-Tadema. The auc-tion-house expert needs to gauge the state of the market before arriving at an auction estimate, and this state of the market will be an important factor in the research necessary to produce a reliable estimate. Our van Goyen is a superb example, in excellent condition, from a great period in the artist's professional life. We are confident that it will fetch twice what the other painting by van Goyen made in New York last January.

What Condition Is This Work In?

Once again, different criteria prevail in different fields, but the general rule remains inviolate. For a work of art to retain its full value, it must be in excellent condition. Repairs, restorations, alterations, and any other activities that remove a work from its original state can only dimin-ish both quality and, thus, value. The skill is in knowing what constitutes good condition. The most difficult issue is detecting highly efficient restoration, not to mention the already-discussed possibility of a supremely competent forgery. As previously mentioned, science can come to the collectors' aid, but the expert learns to perform the most incisive of visual inspections and to trust his or her judg-ment when something looks too good to be true or fails to exhibit wear in the appropriate places. The task becomes most difficult in those areas in which the raw materials are still available. Many are the nightmares that can be told surrounding the efforts of the best furniture repro-ducers. In the late 1960s, an inquiring journalist in London had two Venetian blackamoor torchères created out of a General Post Office telephone pole and then had great fun offering them—with considerable success—to the dealers and auction houses. Condition, about which more will be said, must be questioned early on in the search for accurate evaluation. As already stated, the van Goyen is in great condition, virtually undisturbed since its creation in the seventeenth century.

Has It Been Restored and, If So, How Heavily?

The beginning collector should not expect to be able to detect all elements of restoration, for many of them are so subtle as to be virtually indistinguishable to the naked eye. Bearing in mind the old adage that "it takes one to know one," one of the best pieces of advice is to engage for a reasonable fee a competent and recommended restorer to give an opinion on condition, should the purchase be major and should there be any doubt in the potential buyer's mind. The major auction houses are glad to offer condition reports on any item up for sale, and a request for such a report should be a matter of routine. In addition, in some fields there are easy technical tests that can be applied. The use of the ultraviolet, or "black light," to detect overpainting on a painting is an example of this kind of test, though some experience is necessary to interpret such an inspection and there are varnishes available that more or less neutralize the efficacy of this form of testing. Paper can be dated accurately, and carbon 14 testing can prove highly effective. There is no substitute, however, for learning to spot the ravages of time and unscrupulous restoration with the naked eye. Professional courses are available in most fields, and this is time very well invested. The auction-house expert is ever alert to the issue of condition, maintaining a cynicism when faced with the apparently too perfect and knowing what patina and appearance the dust of the ages should produce. In England, we call this "country-house condition," and it is becoming rarer every day.

What Should the Sales Estimate Be for This Work?

The specialist will have unconsciously made a comparison between the work at hand and previous similar examples. The state of the market will also affect this calculation. All the questions just asked will come into play as the specialist makes an educated guess at the range of price likely to be reached by a particular work of art. Several things need to be remembered in looking at a sales estimate. It is a price *range,* based on the auction house's experience to date. The expert will have a reasonable idea of the least that an item should bring, all things being equal (which, of course, they never are). The market may have changed within the last two months. The buyer of the previous similar lot may no longer be in the bidding. The economy in Japan, Germany, or at home may have suffered a minor change. The sales date may coincide with some event that prevents a buyer from viewing and bidding on a particular lot or sale. At the top end of the estimate, however, there is no way for an auction house to predict with total accuracy the upward potential of a lot. There are the occasions when two bidders become engaged in a determined battle to outbid one another, and then the price becomes an aberration on the upward side, a factor that will be borne in mind when subsequent estimates are created. Given all of these factors, it is interesting to note how accurate most auction estimates turn out to be, and while generalities do not mean much, it is usual for prices to wind up either within the range or within 20 percent of the low or high estimate. What makes auction such a worthwhile medium for sale are those occasions when a new level of price is attained and prices that are even multiples of the high estimate are achieved. This pleases both the consignor and the auction house and ensures that the next similar item will be estimated very differently. Since works by van Goyen appear fairly regularly on the international market, we can be reasonably certain about the accuracy of our estimate.

What Should the Reserve or Minimum Price Be for This Work of Art?

The reserve or minimum is the protective price below which an item offered at auction is not sold. It is a figure that has been agreed on between the consignor and the auctioneer prior to the sale. It is confidential, and the auctioneer may make consecutive bids against other bidders in order to render this minimum effective. The auctioneer may not make these consecutive bids above the reserve, and the reserve is not allowed by law to exceed the low estimate. The auction house does not wish to sell items well below their value, but neither the consignor nor the auctioneer makes any profit if large quantities of lots remain unsold. A general rule of thumb is to set the reserves at 80 percent of the low estimate. In the case of more valuable items—and more aggressive consignors—it is not unusual for the reserve to be at the low estimate. Experience, nevertheless, suggests that reasonable or even low estimates and reserves make for high prices since nothing encourages a bidding audience more than to see the possibility of items selling below the low estimate. This will be particularly true of large multiple properties such as estate consignments. On occasion, a "global" reserve will be set in which the auctioneer is given discretion to apply the overage from one lot to a subsequent lot, while assigning an absolute minimum on each lot. This is of great use in estate sales and large consignments when the purpose is to sell every lot, and it allows for the "swings and roundabouts" nature of the auction itself. A degree of flexibility makes sense. A good expert will give a reasonable initial estimate and will be ready to adjust that estimate on the basis of further research into the work of art and of the response to the work of art from the market prior to the final publication of the estimate in the auction catalogue. The reason that the most expensive items are listed in the catalogue as "Estimate on request" is to allow the department to give informed estimates right up until the day of sale, based on the response of significant potential bidders to the work itself. It is always worth asking the expert how accurate an estimate looks as a sale approaches; the response to this question can be extremely instructive to a potential bidder.

When Is the Next Appropriate Sale?

Timing is a big issue in the world of art auctions. Most departments have two big sales a year and several lesser ones. Items sell best when in the appropriate company. It does not do a minor work of art any favors to place it alongside a masterpiece, and, conversely, it is obviously risky to place a masterpiece in the company of minor decorative works of art. The reason for this is that each sale attracts the buyers at that particular level. We shall suggest placing the van Goyen in the principal sale to be held in New York next January, when it will receive widespread international attention.

A second issue is the balance of a sale in a particular area. There need to be enough examples to attract the regular buyers in the field, but not so many as to give the impression of an oversupply. The major auction houses confer with each other to make sure that major sales coincide, often with important dealer or museum exhibitions or antique shows, thus attracting the greatest number of participants in a given field. The patterns of these offerings are fairly fixed, although subject to some distortion by the appearance of major one-owner sales. The specialists understand the importance of timing, advertising, and marketing, and since they have a major interest in the success of their sales, the advice they offer is well worth attention. The auction market is seasonal, the seasons differing according to international location. It is also true that taste changes internationally and that some markets are stronger than others, depending on the selling site. The specialist will bear all of this in mind as decisions are made, not only as to when the best moment to sell would be, but where a work of art or a collection would sell to the best advantage. There is, for instance, a great deal of difference in the type of jewelry that will sell best in New York, London, Geneva, and Hong Kong. The auction house will advise the consignor in this, as in every aspect of a potential sale.

What the Expert Is Looking For: The Quest for Quality—the Ten Criteria

In the final analysis, what separates two seemingly identical works of art as to value is their differing quality. Having said that, quality can be analyzed to some degree, its component parts enunciated. The acknowledged expert in a field will be quick to suggest that his or her final judgment is based upon "gut reaction," but in reality we can break that reaction down by examining the possibly subconscious criteria that are being applied in order to arrive at an opinion. These ten criteria are not exhaustive and will not always apply. Certainly, their priority and proportion will vary with each field and work of art considered. I would, however, argue that most of them apply most of the time and that reliable expertise will depend on their consideration and application. They constitute, if you will, the general rules by which value in the art market functions.

Authenticity

When we considered the role of the expert, we discussed the need for healthy cynicism when approaching a work of art. Labels, certificates of authenticity, lengthy documentation, and other claims do not in themselves determine authenticity. Signatures are notoriously easy to manufacture or reproduce. The signature on the Frederick Remington bronze (see Figure 4) means nothing if one is

Figure 4. Frederick Remington, *Bronco Buster*

looking at a mass-produced, unlimited, posthumous cast. Of equally little value is the Rembrandt monogram on a *Portrait of Titus* that was appraised for estate purposes in the early 1970s. Donated to a major museum, this painting was not only signed, but appeared in all the major monographs on the artist as an authentic Rembrandt. It was shown in several prestigious exhibitions and had been one of the stars in a noted collection. Upon receipt by the museum, it was sent to the Restoration Department for

a much-needed cleaning. Initial dabs of solvent on the
varnish produced immediate paint loss and the restorer's
suspicion was aroused. Subsequent radiographic photography at the Brookhaven National Laboratory revealed a
nineteenth-century German painting *under* the "Rembrandt." Here, indeed, was an intended fraud.

Figure 5. Joseph Rocca, Stradivarius-style violin

But not all copies are fraudulent; neither are some without value. Take, for example, the "Stradivarius" violin
offered for sale in London in 1993 (see Figure 5). This
instrument was made in the style of Stradivarius and was
of sufficient quality that it might have been passed off as
an original, although a true professional would have been
capable of detecting its lack of age. However, it is well
known that most violins contain a maker's label on the
interior. Certainly, most fake Stradivarii contain fake

INSIDE THE AUCTION HOUSE

Stradivarius labels. This particular violin contained a genuine label that read: "Joseph Rocca fecit Premiato di Med-
aglie alle Esposizione di Torino, Genova, Londre e Parigi,
Taurini, anno Domini 1853 IHS." Thus, we are confronted
by a fine reproduction, from 1853, which realized $121,863
at auction in 1993, as little as a tenth of the price of a
genuine Stradivarius, but still a satisfactory result.

Authenticity may also depend upon documentation.
Many artists' works are included in catalogues raisonnés,
complete listings of the artist's works by a reliable scholar.
It is necessary to determine which scholars are to be relied
upon for a given artist, a determination that is easy to
make by referring to the scholars listed in competent auction catalogues.

In the case of furniture and the decorative arts, designs
and order books may prove instructive. Thus, in considering the Tiffany bowl with turtles, in the Japanese style
(1879), the numbered Tiffany design book shows the ham-
mering and mounting design for this piece, offering the
potential purchaser some comfort but also awakening the
possibility of some unscrupulous forger creating a new
work in the appropriate metals from this readily available
design.

The auction-house expert will know of all the documentary sources in a given area and will come to know the
artists and craftsmen responsible for a work of art so well
that authenticity becomes a less daunting issue. For the
beginner, the reliability of another's expertise becomes a
sine qua non. Such knowledge is worth acquiring even if
it involves considerable expense.

Condition

Good condition is an essential element of quality—and,
thus, of value—and the intelligent collector should never
compromise in this matter. It is important to learn what
constitutes good condition in each area of the fine and

decorative arts. A bronze by Rodin should ideally retain its original patina and, therefore, should not be polished by an overzealous housecleaner. A Paul Revere silver tankard should certainly be cleaned, but not with an abrasive, all-purpose metal cleaner. An old-master painting may need a new coat of varnish once in a generation, but this delicate task should only be undertaken by a highly skilled, qualified painting restorer, whose references should be carefully checked.

Condition can be a prime factor in determining rarity, as in the case of the Honus Wagner baseball card (see Figure 6). Around 1910, the Piedmont Cigarette Company published its Honus Wagner baseball card. There was an immediate problem. The company had failed to consult Mr. Wagner in advance and learned shortly after publication that, way ahead of his day, Wagner objected to cigarette smoking as being unhealthy and demanded that the baseball card be withdrawn from the market and destroyed. Fewer than 40 of the cards survived this recall, and only 10 of them remain in collectible condition. The card illustrated, in better condition than any of the remainder, commanded a price of $410,000 in 1991. It was resold in 1996, achieving a price of $640,500, a further indication of its great rarity and appeal.

Condition plays a major role in most areas of collectibles, and nowhere is it more important than in the realm of toys. When we see high prices recorded for toys that we ourselves enjoyed as children, we wonder if the collecting world has not gone a little crazy. But, as we think further, we begin to understand what this is all about. We did, indeed, enjoy our toys, and there lies the rub. By the time we had finished with them, containers and original condition had become bygone fantasies. Little wonder, then, that the most valuable antique toys are those that remain in their original condition and, better yet, still in their original boxes and wrappings, together with any printed instructions for their use and enjoyment. Thus, "mint and

Figure 6. Honus Wagner baseball card

boxed" is the highest accolade that can be bestowed on an antique plaything. The model of the famous ship *Lusitania* (see Figure 7), while not in its original box, held considerable appeal when it appeared for sale in 1983. The liner itself was built in 1907. The model was manufactured in

Figure 7. Lusitania clockwork battleship

1908 in Germany. The actual liner was sunk by German torpedoes on May 7, 1915, precipitating the United States entry into the First World War. It did the price no harm that Malcolm Forbes collected early mechanical ship models. The *Lusitania* realized $26,000, an amount that could have purchased the collector a small yacht (but he already owned the *Highlander*). The value of the model will continue to appreciate on the basis of its rarity and condition alone.

To move from the minute to the grand, an accurate definition of what constitutes *good condition* in American eighteenth-century furniture is well illustrated by the case of the Philadelphia wing chair (see Figure 8a and b). Visitors to auction exhibitions are sometimes appalled when they come upon what is described as an eighteenth-century masterpiece, its upholstery ripped to shreds and showing evidence of multiple old nail holes. However, it needs to be pointed out that, while great value attaches to the rare occurrence of original upholstery still in good condition, use over the years would normally necessitate reupholstery, probably not more than once every generation in Philadelphia, where profligate spending on maintenance has never been characteristic. The great skill and artistry in this Philadelphia wing chair are not, after all, in the upholstery, but in the form and carving of the frames. Thus, the chair's extraordinary value. But the story is not over yet. This particular wing chair was part of a set executed for the Revolutionary War hero General John Cadwalader. Five side chairs from the same set were found in Ireland and sold in New York in 1974 for $207,500. A further singularity with this set is that, unlike the more prosaic claw-and-ball feet often encountered in chairs of this period, this group of chairs rejoiced in having "hairy paw feet," an extreme and desirable rarity. In addition, the original bill of sale for this chair survives in the Pennsylvania Historical Society, in which "an easy chair to sute [sic] ditto £4.10s. (not including carving)" is listed. Given the

Figure 8a and b. Philadelphia Cadwalader
wing chair

very limited supply and the burgeoning demand for such historic examples of American furniture from this, the finest, period of manufacture, the price of $2.75 million in January 1987, is astonishing but explicable.

Figure 9. Nantucket nesting baskets

Rarity

Rarity alone may create value, but there are limits: an item may be so rare that it falls outside any collecting area, and transactions may be sufficiently infrequent as to deter potential purchasers. However, rarity combined with other qualities usually produce extremely high value, as the examples that follow will attest.

Visitors to Nantucket continue to enjoy the opportunity of acquiring either a single "lightship" basket or, better yet, a nesting set. They will discover that even the recent baskets do not come cheap. No surprise, then, that a complete set of baskets from the nineteenth century (see Figure 9) would command a stellar price. Coupled with its inclusion in a premier collection, that of Bertram K. and Nina Fletcher Little, this set of six nesting baskets, labeled Davis Hall, fetched $118,000 in the Little Sale in 1994. Rarity must be considered the predominant citerion in this instance, though one should not forget the superb condition, the identification of the maker, and the pure aesthetic beauty of these wonderful creations.

Rarity is once again the prime explanation for the price of the Korean painting in ink, color, and gold on silk from the Koryo dynasty of the late fourteenth century (see Figure 10). This subject, *The Water Moon—Avalokitervana*, when it appeared in 1991 caused great excitement since there were no known examples extant in Korea. Coupled with the recent rapid improvement in Korea's economy and the availability of considerable wealth to repurchase its patrimony, all elements combined to produce an extraordinary result. Previous sales of similar, but not identical, works led the specialist in charge of the sale to place a presale estimate of $150,000 to $200,000 on this item. Showing the advantage of selling at auction, where the price is not in any way limited by the presale estimate and where the upside potential can exceed any previous price level, this work actually fetched $1.76 million and still has not returned to its native land.

In the late eighteenth century, most Americans were too preoccupied to worry about the complicated business of porcelain manufacture. Indeed, America's first and only eighteenth-century porcelain factory was that of Bonnin & Morris, which flourished for only two years, from 1770 to 1772, after which it was put out of business by a flood of cheap imports, but not before it had produced the porcelain, shell-form sweetmeat stand (see Figure 11). This work was purchased for $4 at a Long Island tag sale. When it came to auction sale in 1982, it was one of three known, the other two residing in the Brooklyn Museum and the Smithsonian. This extreme rarity accounted for the sale price of $66,000.

On occasion, rarity is combined with some association that elevates value in an object whose intrinsic worth is minimal. Here, again, documentation is essential, as in the example of *Rosebud*, the sled from the film *Citizen Kane* (see Figure 12). At one level, we are faced by a prop from

Figure 10. Koryo dynasty painting

a commercial film production. At another level, we are presented with an icon from American movie history. In 1982, the sled fetched $55,000.

In 1973, when I was head of Sotheby's Appraisal Company, I received a call from Elizabeth Seton College in

Figure 11. Bonnin & Morris sweetmeat stand

Yonkers, requesting that I make an initial visit to assess the possible value of a collection of old-master paintings that had been left to the college as part of the contents of the William Boyce Thompson mansion, which formed the core of the campus. My inspection of the old-master paintings revealed that they had been extremely heavily restored by the nuns over the years in an amateur attempt to preserve their integrity. They were left without any material value. At the conciliarity tea during which I was passing on this disappointing news, my eye was drawn to a small sugar bowl (see Figure 13a). Experts are notorious for turning objects upside down in order to see if there are identifying marks on the underneath. What appeared to be eighteenth-century export blue-and-white porcelain bore an unusual mark (see Figure 13b). The dome is in fact the Duomo of Florence, and "F" identifies Firenze. There was nothing oriental about this piece other than its style. I made a hasty call to the then-head of Sotheby's Porcelain Department in New York. He was sufficiently excited by what I described to drive back to the college with me that afternoon. He confirmed his suspicion that what I had

Figure 12. Rosebud sled from Citizen Kane

Figure 13a and b. Medici bowl

found was a piece of Medici porcelain. At the end of the sixteenth century, the Medici family had commissioned a factory in Florence to attempt to manufacture porcelain in the oriental method and style. Only some 54 pieces survive that short-lived experiment. In 1973, only 2 remained in private hands. This particular bowl had been sold to Thompson in November 1916 in the sale of the Volpi-Davanzati Palace Collection, lot 625, realizing $200. The nuns sat in the front row of Parke-Bernet Galleries in full habit, twiddling their prayer beads in anticipation of divine assistance as their sugar bowl was sold for $180,000 a truly remarkable price for the time.

The Medici family, great patrons of art, continues to provide the market with a magic aura. In January of 1995, the New-York Historical Society offered some highlights of their European works of art for sale. One of the leading paintings in the group was the "birth salver" created to celebrate the birth of Lorenzo de' Medici (see Figure 14a and b). This piece, by Giovanni di Ser Giovanni di Simone, called Lo Scheggia, who worked in the sixteenth century, is not only rare in form—a birthplate—but is in amazingly good condition for its age. Add to this the historical association, provenance, and documentation, and all the ingredients for a great sale are in place. Finally, the painting was bought by the Metropolitan Museum, where it had been on loan since 1979. They wanted "their" painting back. All these conditions combined to produce a price of $2 million. It seemed not inappropriate that the title of this work was *The Triumph of Fame*.

By the beginning of the nineteenth century, German immigrants in Virginia had begun to produce their own stylistic versions of furniture and decorations that combined their Teutonic background with the local traditions of the Shenandoah Valley. One such example was the paint-decorated pine dower chest, attributed to Johannes Spitler, from Shenandoah County, Virginia, circa 1800 (see Figure 15). Not only was this chest one of the few known

Figure 14a and b. Giovanni di Ser Giovanni di Simone, called Lo Scheggia, birth salver

examples by this craftsman, but its geometric style was an important precursor to the styles of today. It is in wonderful condition and came up for sale at an auction conducted on site in Virginia in which the collection of Dr. and Mrs. Henry Deyerle was offered. Once again, a conservative presale estimate of $40,000 to $60,000 reflected past expe-

Figure 15. Johannes Spitler, dower chest

rience but did not account for the enthusiasm of the native Virginians who bought this historic piece for $343,500.

It is generally acknowledged that blue-period works are the most sought-after of all of Picasso's oeuvre. Only a handful of major works from this period remain in private collections. Thus, when his *Angel Fernandez De Soto* (see Figure 2, p. 20) came to the market in 1995, bidding was likely to be strong. Additional factors drove this price up. De Soto was a personal friend of Picasso and was characterized as "an amusing wastrel" who eked out a living as an extra at small Parisian theaters, his lifestyle typifying the popular vision of bohemian Paris at the turn of the century. Moreover, the eventual buyer, Sir Andrew Lloyd Webber, not only was particularly fascinated with the connection between the Pre-Raphaelites and Picasso's blue period, but also enjoyed extensive means with which to satisfy his interest. The $29 million paid in 1995 for this work of 1903 makes sense once the context is understood.

Figure 16. Pablo Picasso, *Yo Picasso*

A comparison with the early self-portrait of 1901, *Yo Picasso* (see Figure 16), which sold for $5.83 million in 1981 and resold in 1989 for $47.85 million, demonstrates the movement in this market between these years and proves that the appreciation of the very rarest and best works far outpaces the performance of less extraordinary works.

Historical Importance

More than in any other area, the need for documentation dominates this criterion. It is not enough that George Washington is said to have slept in a bed. There must be documentary evidence of the first president's having visited the house in which the bed is found. His own extensive correspondence can be useful in establishing such proof. American historical material tends to achieve remarkable results at auction. This has to do with the elemental law of supply and demand. American history is relatively short, and the current population that is willing and able to collect the material is vast. Thus, when a document by a historic figure, especially when the subject of the document has intrinsic interest, comes to the market, major prices can be anticipated. Such was the case with Washington's Letter to Henry Knox, a draft of a letter, signed at Mount Vernon on April 1, 1789, in which Washington expressed his doubts and reluctance on the eve of assuming the office of first president of the United States, including the following sentence: "My movements to the chair of government will be accompanied by feelings not unlike those of a culprit who is going to the place of his execution" (see Figure 17). The first president's lack of confidence was misplaced, and this souvenir of that historic moment fetched $635,000 in November 1993.

If the first president commands great interest, it stands to reason that the much-loved first ambassador to Paris would not lag far behind. While in Paris, Benjamin Franklin sat for a portrait bust by Jean-Antoine Houdon, the noted sculptor-portraitist of such luminaries as Voltaire, Washington, Jefferson, and Mirabeau. The result was a remarkable likeness, which appeared for sale in the bicentennial year of 1976, thus creating a wave of patriotic fervor in the salesroom when the British Rail Pension Fund purchased the sculpture for the then high price of $310,000 (see Figure 18). At that time, a bust of an unknown sitter might have reached $30,000. Such is the value of history

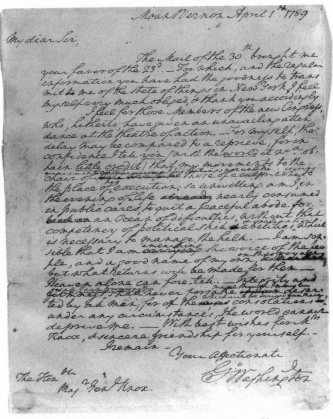

Figure 17. George Washington, letter to Henry Knox

in the auction room. In December 1996, the bust was resold for $2.9 million.

Documentation was once again the key in the case of the gold Freedom Box presented to John Jay by the city of

New York (see Figure 19). This small presentation box, a mere 3⅜ inches long, contained the original document of presentation, complete with ribbon and seal, as well as the incised statement of the purpose of the presentation,

Figure 18. Jean-Antoine Houdon, *Benjamin Franklin*

Figure 19. Samuel Johnson (maker) and Peter Rushton Maverick (engraver), gold Freedom Box presented to John Jay

confirming its historical importance. The maker's mark of Samuel Johnson confirms its manufacture in New York in 1784, and Peter Rushton Maverick added his signature as a result of his role in engraving this historic artifact, which changed hands at $460,000.

Figure 20. Abraham Lincoln's hat and binoculars

There can hardly be a better-known event than Lincoln's fatal trip to Ford's Theatre. Due to unusually full documentation, the sale of the beaver hat he wore on that occasion and the binoculars he used was a considerable success in 1979, when the hat sold for $10,000 and the glasses for $24,000 (see Figure 20). These items, however, lacked the seriousness or attraction of an important historical document such as the autograph leaf from Lincoln's speech on "a house divided" (see Figure 21), which sold in 1992 for $1.4 million. This leaf can be considered the most historically important autograph manuscript to have been discovered this century. The speech was written in late December 1857, as Lincoln was beginning to achieve national recognition. This is his earliest reference to his "house divided" doctrine. The leaf was a survival from the Grimsley Carpet Bag, most of the contents of which were dispersed following Lincoln's death. This particular leaf had been kept by a member of the Elizabeth Todd Grimsley family, providing an important link in the document's provenance.

History continues to be created, and the auction rooms are quick to acknowledge new claimants to the role of historic material. Such was the sale of Russian space equipment, including the *Voskhod* 2 Berkut space suit worn by Alexei Leonov prior to the first Russian spacewalk on March 18, 1965 (see Figure 22). The breaking down of the barrier between the two nations and the dismantling of the USSR made possible the sale of this material and freed Americans to invest in the sale. The suit sold for $255,000, which presumably does not come close to its original cost to the government of the Soviet Union but is not a bad price for secondhand clothing.

Cornelius Van der Burgh may not be the most famous of American silversmiths—Paul Revere undoubtedly can lay claim to that title—but he had another distinction. He was the first native silversmith to operate in the New World. Born in New York in 1652, in 1690 he created a silver double-handled bowl (see Figure 23). This relatively small bowl, 9 inches in diameter, nevertheless occupies an important niche in the history of American artifacts, far surpassing its presale estimate of $100,000 to $150,000 when it sold in 1993 for $210,000.

Why, Kansas is neither the whole, nor a tithe of the real question—

"A house divided against itself can not stand"

I believe this government can not endure permanently, half slave, and half free—

I expressed this belief a year ago; and subsequent developements have but confirmed me.

I do not expect the Union to be dissolved—I do not expect the house to fall; but I do expect it will cease to be divided—It will become all one thing, or all the other—Either the opponents of slavery will arrest the further spread of it, and put it in course of ultimate extinction; or its advocates will push it forward till it shall become alike lawful in all the states, old, as well as new—Do you doubt it? Study the Dred Scott decision, and then see, how little, even now, remains to be done—

That decision may be reduced to three points— The first is, that a negro can not be a citizen— That point is made in order to deprive the negro in every possible event, of the benefit of that provision of the U.S. Constitution which declares that;

"The citizens of each State shall be entitled to all priviliges and immunities of citizens in the several States"

The second point is, that the U.S. Constitution protects slavery, as property, in all the U.S. territories, and that neither congress, nor the people of the territories, nor any other power, can prohibit it, at any time prior to the formation of State constitutions—

This point is made, in order that the territories may safely be filled up with slaves, before the formation of State constitutions, and thereby to embarras the free state

Provenance

Not only can historical importance of a work of art add substantially to its value, but the importance of the owner of a work of art may also have a significant effect.

Figure 22. Russian space suit

In 1783, during the reign of Louis XVI, the monarch commissioned the Sèvres porcelain factory to create a dinner service of 422 pieces, which was manufactured over a twenty-three-year period. By January 1793, when Louis went to the guillotine, about half of the service had been made, the majority of which is now in the British Royal

Collection. Thus, pieces appear on the market with the utmost rarity. In 1986, three pieces did appear, a *seau à demi-bouteille* and two *seaux à verre* (see Figure 24). They all bore the interlaced L's and were dated 1792, 1786, and 1791. They were painted with scenes from classical mythology by Charles-Nicolas Dodin and gilded by Pierre-

Figure 23. Cornelius Van der Burgh, silver bowl

André le Guay. The royal provenance led to a sales price of $227,150, which in the world of porcelain is astronomical.

In 1958, a fine French eighteenth-century console table was sold in New York for the then high price of $40,000 (see Figure 25). The ormulu-mounted, purpleheart and kingwood console was made by J.-H. Riesener, a leading cabinetmaker who rejoiced in the title "Ébèniste Ordinaire du Roi." There was nothing ordinary about his craftsmanship, and his work was almost exclusively performed for the palace of Versailles. As it happened, this console table was commissioned for Marie Antoinette's private suite, or *cabinet intérieur*. The furniture expert at Sotheby's, in inspecting the piece when it reappeared for sale, noticed an inventory mark on the underside of the shelf that he

Figure 24. Sèvres garniture

recognized from his studies as being the actual Versailles inventory number. This unassailable royal identification led to a sales price of $400,000 the second time around, only fourteen years after the sale at $40,000. The supreme quality of this table is reflected in the price of $3.184 million, achieved on its third appearance at auction in 1988.

Ownership does not always confer value directly, but on occasion the taste of a collector can draw attention to an object's rare qualities. In 1986, a rare Attic marble figure of a goddess (see Figure 26) from the late Middle Neolithic period, circa 5000 B.C., was offered for sale from the collection of James Johnson Sweeney, a celebrated museum curator who had gained prominence as director of, first, the Houston Museum of Fine Arts and, later, the Whitney Museum of American Art. Only 42 anthropomorphic figures survive, as opposed to the more common "slab" figures, and only 7 seated female forms are known to exist.

Mr. Sweeney had the good taste to have selected this most rare of forms, and his estate saw the wisdom of his choice when the Cycladic marble figure fetched $1.32 million. The provenance had an important role to play in this price.

Figure 25. J.-H. Riesener, console table

One should not ignore the power of Hollywood when it comes to provenance, and no name carries more magic than that of Elizabeth Taylor. If she could be described as royalty within the film world, it is, therefore, a natural when she herself is tempted by items with a previous royal connection. Such was the case with the plume-of-feathers brooch, which is the symbol of the Prince of Wales and which Miss Taylor purchased from the sale of jewelry belonging to the Duchess of Windsor (see Figure 27). The connection was responsible for the price of $566,610. Much less expensive, but equally royal, was the famous pearl, *La Peregrina,* which Miss Taylor purchased in 1966 for $37,000 (see Figure 28). This antique pearl was discovered in Panama in the sixteenth century, given to Philip II of Spain, who then gave it to Mary I of England. At her death, Philip reclaimed it, a seemingly ungenerous gesture, but it should be remembered that an entire military

Figure 26. Attic marble figure of a goddess

campaign could be financed by the sale of one such pearl in this period. This very pearl appears in several paintings by Velázquez. Few items of jewelry can boast such a romantic royal past.

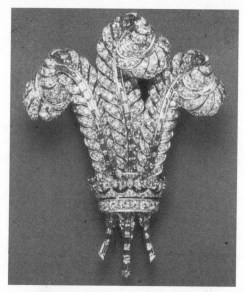

Figure 27. Plume-of-feathers brooch

Figure 28. La Peregrina pearl

It stands to reason that while Elizabeth Taylor is interested in former royal possessions, the market is also interested in Elizabeth Taylor. When her Rolls-Royce came up for auction in 1994, it went way beyond its book value in selling for $508,000 (see Figure 29). Prices are relative in

Figure 29. Elizabeth Taylor's Rolls-Royce

Figure 30. The Beatles' Rolls-Royce

every market, and popularity becomes a factor in the sale of items with celebrity provenance. It, thus, makes sense that the Beatles' Rolls-Royce, an icon of the psychedelic 1960s, would outperform Miss Taylor's vehicle, which it did substantially when it appeared in New York in 1985 (see Figure 30). John Lennon purchased a standard 1965 Rolls-Royce Phantom V Touring Limousine, with Mulliner Park Ward coachwork in 1966. Lennon then had "a

Figure 31. Elton John memorabilia

mystic friend" from Weybridge, in Surrey, England, paint the car to his own specifications, producing the spectacular result seen in Figure 31. The car was eventually donated to the Cooper-Hewitt Museum, which did not have adequate space to display it. The car was offered for auction to benefit the museum in 1985, with an estimate of $200,000 to $300,000, astonishing the world with its eventual sale at $2.9 million.

Popular musicians, with their broad range of support, continue to attract high prices. A selection of Elton John's costumes and memorabilia bear this fact out (see Figure 31). The items in Figure 32 realized an aggregate of $23,100 in 1988, clear evidence that fame has a value completely unrelated to intrinsic worth, a conclusion that was reiterated with the sale of a group of cookie jars from the collection of Andy Warhol (see Figure 32), which commanded a total of $247,000 in the same year. Mr. Warhol's fame outlasted his prescribed fifteen minutes.

Size

"The bigger, the better" is not necessarily the case when it comes to works of art. Extremes of size can be complicated. A Renoir oil that measures 3 inches square will not give the owner quite the psychic reward that a full-scale canvas might. A 20-foot-high painting by Albert Bierstadt, *The Yosemite,* may be magnificent, but its size will prevent most private collectors from bidding on it. If, however, the quality is outstanding, size may not be as great a detraction as might be supposed. In the matter of size, various areas of art are affected differently.

In the realm of gemstones, providing that clarity is present in a flawless stone, "the bigger, the better" applies, as evidenced in the perfect pear-shaped diamond of classical unmodified cut, D flawless, weighing in at 100.1 carats, and selling in Geneva in 1995 for $15,416,666. As is the tradition with large unmounted stones, the buyer is entitled to rename his purchase, and on this occasion the stone was aptly renamed the Star of the Season (see Figure 33).

In 1863, Frederick Edwin Church brought his latest and one of his largest paintings, *The Icebergs,* to London for a special exhibition (see Figure 34). Following the exhibition, he sold the painting to Sir Edward Watkin, a northern English businessman and railroad magnate, who removed the work to his large mansion in Manchester, where it hung until its rediscovery in June of 1979. Over the years, the mansion experienced various uses and fi-

Figure 32. Andy Warhol's cookie jars

nally became a convalescent home, run by the Social Services Department of the city of Manchester. The residents
gained no pleasure from the vast and by then dark sea-
scape that loomed over them on an upper stairway hall.
The painting was removed to facilitate the repainting of
the hallway, and Sotheby's was contacted. Once the old
varnish was removed, the masterpiece became evident.

Figure 33. Star of the Season diamond

Figure 34. Frederick Edwin Church, *Icebergs*

The vast size, $64\frac{1}{4} \times 112\frac{1}{4}$ inches without the frame, proved no distraction, as the bidding reached $2.5 million in 1979. This masterpiece is now on view at the Dallas Museum of Art.

At the other end of the scale, diminutive size may not rule out high value in the case of works of exquisite quality. Such was the case with Leonardo da Vinci's two-sided sheet of studies, which includes a possible study of *Saint John the Baptist with the Lamb*, a study of machinery, and an old man, together with a sample of Leonardo's famous "mirror writing," measuring $8 \times 5\frac{7}{16}$ inches (see Figure 35). The drawing came with the highly significant provenance of Sir Thomas Lawrence, King William II of Holland, and the Grand Ducal Collection from the Schlossmuseum in Weimar. Such was the quality and the rarity of this work that it fetched $3.63 million and now resides in the J. Paul Getty Museum in Malibu.

Equally diminutive but of utmost quality and in extraordinary condition for a work of art from the fifteenth century was Rogier van der Weyden's *Saint George and the Dragon*, sold in London in 1966 (see Figure 36). While Sotheby's catalogued it as the work of Hubert van Eyck, a brother of the better known Jan van Eyck, the attribution was not so much the issue as the quality. There are even some scholars who doubt the very existence of Hubert. This did not deter the National Gallery of Art in Washington, D.C., who bought the work for $660,000, and it can now be viewed, through a magnifying glass, in a special case created for it, in the nation's capital.

Medium

The actual materials in which a work of art is created can have a significant effect upon its value. Thus, an original oil by Rembrandt is likely to be more valuable than a drawing by him, and the drawing will be more valuable than a print, all things being equal. This is not to say that

an extremely fine and important drawing may not on occasion prove more valuable than a damaged small early
painting, or that a perfect rendition of the *Hundred Guilder*
print might not command a higher price than a slight and

Figure 35. Leonardo da Vinci, sheet of studies

unremarkable drawing. The law of supply and demand continues to operate. It must also be said that some media are simply more popular than others. For example, pastels are not sought after by many collectors partly because of

Figure 36. Rogier van der Weyden, *Saint George and the Dragon*

Figure 37. Gilbert Stuart, *George Washington*

Figure 38. One-dollar bill

their vulnerability to damage through climate and movement. Exceptions can be found in individual artists, as in the case of Degas, Cassatt, and William Meritt Chase, to name three notable examples.

Not only the medium, but the place within an artist's oeuvre must be considered. Thus, the unfinished portrait of George Washington painted by Gilbert Stuart on April 12, 1796 (the artist's daughter Charlotte has described the sitting), is intensely valuable because it was the *first* of the many versions that the artist painted of this illustrious subject and will always outperform the unlimited-edition print still being produced by the U.S. Treasury after this original painting (see Figures 37 and 38).

In their etched form, Pierre-Joseph Redouté's illustrations of the various specimens of the lily family must rank second only to his studies of roses for recognition and popularity. It stands to reason, then, that the original watercolor drawings would have extraordinary value, and such is the case. When 468 original drawings, complete with a unique printing of the text, appeared on the market in 1985, the response was predictable. As Fanny Mallary expressed it in *Art at Auction, 1985–86* (p. 182): "Occasionally a work of art comes onto the market which combines high quality, historical and artistic importance, illustrious provenance and sheer beauty." Such was the case with *Les Liliacées*, which had been bought from the artist by the

Empress Josephine and sold at auction for $5.5 million (see Figure 39).

Irises fare well at auction. There can be few who are unaware of the record price fetched for van Gogh's incom-

Figure 39. Pierre-Joseph Redouté, *Les Liliacées*

parable oil of this subject, which sold at the very height of the market in 1987 for $53.9 million (see Figure 40). The painting had been bought by its first owner, Octave Mirbeau, for Fr 250 and entered the collection of Joan Whitney

Payson in 1947, the postwar period in which major paintings changed hands at comparatively nominal prices. It now graces the collection of the Getty Museum. In van Gogh's case, the oil paintings remain infinitely more valuable than the works in other media.

Figure 40. Vincent van Gogh, *Irises*

Carl Fabergé's workshop was renowned for working in precious metals and gemstones. The medium itself has intrinsic value, but this value became greatly magnified when Fabergé's work masters transformed the materials into unique gifts, most especially those gifts commissioned by the czar for his own family. The imperial Russian Easter eggs, of which only 54 examples are known to survive, are the epitome of this craft. Rare materials in rare objects with an extremely limited supply and a royal connection combine to account for the high value accorded these fascinating works, all of which go to explain the $3.19 million paid for the *Love Trophy* egg created by work master Henrik Wigstrom in St. Petersburg circa 1905 (see Figure 41).

Figure 41. Carl Fabergé, *Love Trophy* egg

Subject Matter

There is no question that the subject matter of a work of art can have significant effect upon its desirability and, hence, its value. While it should be emphasized that the collector is encouraged to buy only what she or he likes, the collector should at the same time be aware of general taste as it relates to subject matter and, in doing so, recognize the subtle nuances that can obtain in subjects that might even appear to be similar, if not identical. James Joseph Jacques Tissot's subject, *Le Banc de Jardin* (see Figure 42), is not only a superb example of the artist's work, the subject is irresistable, accounting for the staggering price of $5.28 million in 1994, at which time the previous auction record for Tissot was $3.08 million. The reverse

Figure 42. James Joseph Jacques Tissot, *Le Banc de Jardin*

obtains with Monet's *Faisans, Bécasses, et Perdrix* (see Figure 43). Even though a fine example of the artist's work, there can be no denying that there are many collectors who would prefer not to gaze upon a group of dead birds on a daily basis.

On occasion, an unusual subject or an unusual treatment of a subject can have a positive effect upon a work of art's value. Annibale Carracci's *Boy Drinking* displayed this characteristic (see Figure 44). Executed in the early 1580s, this evocation of a moment captured in time, portrayed from an unusual perspective, demands the viewer's attention and was a highlight from the sale of the collection of Peter Sharp when it sold in 1994 for $2.2 million.

To underline my theory that seemingly identical works may differ considerably in value, let us take the example of Winslow Homer's watercolors, in which we can con-

Figure 43. Claude Monet, *Faisans, Bécasses, et Perdrix*

sider four works (see Figures 45–48). Figures 45 and 46 appear to be identical: they are the same medium, watercolor; they are the same size; they were painted around the same time; they are both signed; the subject is identical, two boys in a boat. And yet Figure 45 failed to sell at $72,500, and Figure 46 fetched $150,000. The difference— and it is an important one—is that in the second work

Figure 44. Annibale Carracci, *Boy Drinking*

the boys are in a calm sea. The viewer feels much more comfortable. In Figure 47, the boys are safely on the shore in a similarly idyllic seaside setting, and our logic holds good. The watercolor fetched $270,000, granted in a

Figure 45. Winslow Homer, *Two Boys in a Boat*

Figure 46. Winslow Homer, *Two Boys in a Boat*

strengthening market. So what is Figure 48 going to realize? A rough sea and no charming children? Yes, but we
are here dealing with much more of a major work of art,
which is the artist's last dated watercolor, showing his
final achievement in a medium that he strongly favored
and illustrating his fascination with the theme of man
against nature, as the sales-catalogue entry notes: "The

Figure 47. Winslow Homer, *Boys on the Beach*

Figure 48. Winslow Homer, *Diamond Shoal*

striking beauty of the image, dramatically rendered with a vibrant palette, belies the implicit danger of Homer's portrayal of man's epic struggle against the sea. In *Diamond Shoal,* Homer captures the tension of the two men struggling to regain control of their sailboat in the face of the unpredictable forces of nature." Could it be that we are less concerned about this danger when adults are involved, based on our confidence that these weather-worn sailors will have the skill to master the situation? And does not the presence of the Diamond Shoal lightship offer us further comfort? The specialist will not, therefore, be surprised to learn that this fourth watercolor fetched $1.8 million, when sold by the IBM Collection in 1995. In the computerized price listing, all four could appear as "Winslow Homer, *Seascape, Watercolor, Signed.*" Let the collector beware.

Frank W. Benson's contribution to American impressionism could hardly be compared with that of Childe Hassam or William Merritt Chase, and his portraiture does not always match the élan of John Singer Sargent. But in one of his works, *The Sisters* (see Figure 49), he surpassed himself in capturing the total delight of two children in a charming summer setting. Here, the subject is everything. Sheila Dugan, who is preparing the catalogue raisonné for the artist, is quoted in the catalogue of the IBM sale at Sotheby's as follows: "*The Sisters* is at once typical and unique in Benson's oeuvre. As a depiction of idyllic childhood it remains unsurpassed. . . . If Frank Benson had any doubts about the popularity of *The Sisters* they were dispelled in the spring of 1901 when the canvas was shown at the annual *Ten American Painters* Exhibition at New York's Durand-Ruel Galleries. Rarely would the artist receive such glowing reviews. The painting was applauded by critics for its brilliant brushwork and handling of outdoor light, and its lovely depiction of childhood. . . . Nearly one hundred years ago the timeless appeal of *The Sisters* was articulated by the critic William Howe Downes

... "I would be at a loss to find a more sympathetic, intimate, charming representation of human babyhood." It did no harm to the painting's reputation that the children involved were the artist's own daughters, Elizabeth and Sylvia. The sale price of $4.2 million is no guarantee that

Figure 49. Frank W. Benson, *The Sisters*

the next work by Benson to come on the market will even fetch $100,000. Subject must be taken seriously in assessing the value of a work of art.

Fashion

At any given time, it is not easy to determine those areas of collecting that are the subject of immediate fashion rather than destined to maintain their value over the long haul. Taste changes, and it has long been my private theory that taste in art skips generations. I believe this is a psychological phenomenon based on the fact that most people have fond memories of their grandparents and the possessions that surrounded them, whereas children and parents tend to differ in their taste. It has been said, perhaps only half in jest, that the link between grandparents and grandchildren is that they have a common enemy. Whether my pet theory holds any water or not, taste in collecting certainly changes, and the wary collector keeps an eye on movements within his or her general field.

In the early 1980s, the world record for a piece of American furniture, a Chippendale shell-carved block-front mahogany kneehole desk by the Goddard-Townsend family of Newport, Rhode Island, was the same as the record for the wisteria lamp by Tiffany and Company: $360,000 (see Figures 50 and 51). I remember commenting that the eighteenth-century piece of furniture would surely increase in value at a more rapid rate than the circa-1900 artifact. I now have to admit that I was partially wrong in that the taste for Tiffany lamps has not abated in spite of some fluctuations. In 1995, the Favrile glass-bead and bronze Virginia creeper lamp (see Figure 52) brought $1.1 million. However, I was right about American eighteenth-century furniture, in which area the world record at auction was recently increased by the Newport John Brown desk that sold for $12 million.

I might have made similar remarks about the taste for the art of the English classical painter Sir Lawrence Alma-Tadema, whose works were avidly collected by the television producer Allen Funt in the late 1960s and early 1970s. He offered his whole collection for sale in November 1973, and his *Baths of Caracalla* sold at that time for $38,000 (see Figure 53). Reoffered for sale in 1993, this same work sold for $2.42 million. Once again, what I would have de-

Figure 50. Goddard-Townsend family, kneehole desk

Figure 51. Tiffany, wisteria lamp

scribed as a passing fashion appears to have acquired a degree of permanence that cannot be ignored.

Quality

This final criterion is the most elusive and yet in many ways sums up the other nine. For it is, in the final analysis,

Figure 52. Tiffany, Virginia creeper lamp

the *quality* of a work of art that will determine its ultimate value. The encouraging result of this is that in the presence of a work of art of undoubted quality, the art market will tend to respond appropriately. In other words, while there are subjective elements in the determination of what constitutes quality, a consensus will arise among experts as to

Figure 53. Sir Lawrence Alma-Tadema, *Baths of Caracalla*

the superior quality of a given work of art. Be it van Gogh's *Irises* or Rogier van der Weyden's *Saint George and the Dragon,* J.-H. Riesener's console table or a group of nesting lightship baskets from Nantucket, collectors agree that they are presented with works of enduring, supreme quality, and major prices are achieved in the auction room. At its best, this standard of quality will move the collector, as one is moved by an extraordinary piece of music, a breathtaking view in nature, or the onset of a loving relationship. True quality must produce passion, the key element in successful collecting. Many of the items discussed in this chapter exhibit that superior quality. I have, however, selected four additional works to underline this most important criterion.

Demonstrating that quality can overrule size, a small masterpiece by Raphaelle Peale, *Still Life with Raisin Cake,* measuring 8×11 inches, was my favorite from a group of American still-life paintings from the collection of Donald and Jean Stralem (see Figure 54). To realize that this deceptively simple still life was painted in 1813 renders it all the more unusual since its composition, while owing much to the compositions of the prime exponents of still-life painting in Holland in the seventeenth-century, also acts as a precursor to Manet's still-life subjects of more than fifty years later. This delectable confection reached $354,000 at the sale in May of 1995.

We have already taken a look at the work of Carl Fabergé's masters in the use of precious metals and jewels. But since these works summarize the ideal of quality, I was unable to resist the inclusion of a second imperial Easter egg (see Figure 55). This imperial version of the lowlier cuckoo clock is referred to by A. Kenneth Snowman in his comprehensive work, *The Art of Carl Fabergé* (Greenwich, Conn.: New York Graphic Society, 1975), as the *Chanticleer Egg,* probably presented to the dowager empress Marie Feodorovna by Nicholas II in 1903. As Snowman describes the clock's action: "The diamond-set cockerel in gold and varicolored enamels which rises from the interior of the egg, flapping its wings and crowing, does not do so at the pressure of a button, but automatically at each hour. When it has announced the time, it disappears beneath the grille which closes down over the top of the egg." In 1985, this wonderful combination of Easter egg, clock, and mechanical toy brought $1.6 million at auction.

Figure 54. Raphaelle Peale, *Still Life with Raisin Cake*

George Bellows has long been admired as a great chronicler of Americana and particularly for his treatment of classic boxing scenes. Occasionally, an artist will surpass himself, as was suggested in the case of Frank W. Benson. There is little question that Bellows falls into this category in the case of his *Easter Snow, 1915* (see Figure 56). This evocative view of Riverside Park under a late snow with the Hudson River in the background displays Bellows at his fullest vigor, making bold experiments with color and indulging in his broadest and most assured brushwork. The price of $2.8 million in 1995 set a new record for Bellows, a price that may remain his record for a time since works of such outstanding quality by this artist seldom appear on the open market.

My final example of supreme quality is that of Henri Matisse's *La Pose Hindoue* of 1923 (see Figure 57), described in the catalogue as "one of the most abstract, both in the symmetrical pose of the model and the flat pat-

Figure 55. Carl Fabergé, cuckoo clock

terning of the interior in which she is seated," of all Matisse's odalisques. Jack Cowart is quoted in the catalogue notes as follows: "The season 1922–23 is characterized by a series of single-figure portraits. The model was Henriette, set—almost wedged—against decorative backgrounds. Their stylistic evolution toward dramatic abstraction can be seen in a group of four odalisques. . . .

Figure 56. George Bellows, *Easter Snow, 1915*

The last of this painting group is *La Pose Hindoue*, a work intimate yet of monumental visual proportions. Here Henriette is shown cross-legged, static like an Eastern icon, hands above head; strong flat patterns of the chair drapery, window shutters, wallpaper, and hangings tightly lock in the remaining canvas area. The contrasts of abstracted form and colors are clear. It is the rigorous simplifications of works like this that launch his highly stylized paintings of the 1930s" (Jack Cowart, "The Place of Silvered Light: An Expanded, Illustrated Chronology of

Matisse in the South of France," in *Henri Matisse: The Early Years in Nice,* [Washington, D.C.: National Gallery of Art, 1986–87], pp. 30–32). This wonderful painting not only stands on its own as a superlative work by a great master, but provides a fascinating example of an artist in transition. Its auction price of $14.85 million in 1995 bore testimony to its quality, its attraction, and its greatness.

Figure 57. Henri Matisse, *La Pose Hindoue*

The Creation of a Sale

A major auction room such as Sotheby's will maintain a wide variety of departments in order to meet the needs of most clients immediately. The sales catalogues give a listing of the expert departments, together with the names of the experts. This listing helps to dispel the misimpression that the major auction room is only interested in multimillion-dollar works of art.

At Sotheby's, the area of painting is divided into seven departments: American; Impressionist and Modern; Contemporary; Latin American; Nineteenth Century; Old Master Paintings; and Chinese. Sotheby's also boasts the following departments: Old Master and Modern Prints; Contemporary Prints; and Photographs.

Furniture and decorations are similarly subdivided into American Decorative Arts and Furniture; American Folk Art; English Furniture; European Furniture; European Works of Art and Tapestries; Nineteenth Century Furniture, Decorations, and Works of Art; and Art Deco and Art Nouveau. These seven departments are supplemented by departments specializing in Antiquities; Arms and Armor; Collectibles; Paperweights; Porcelain; Rugs and Carpets; Silver; Watches, Clocks, and Scientific Instruments.

The Jewelry Department represents one of the largest contributors to our annual sales, orchestrating sales and exhibitions in locations all over the world; it is subdivided into Antique and Modern sections, with another department specializing in the Oriental market.

Other fields represented are those involving Oriental, Asian and Islamic Works of Art, often subdivided into particular countries such as Korea. Pre-Columbian Art has its own department, as does North American Indian, African, and Oceanic Art, as well as Judaica. We should not forget the major contribution made to our business by the Book Department, a survivor from our founding and the repository of extensive and much-respected scholarship. More surprising to the uninitiated might be the departments that deal with Animation and Comic Art; Coins; Stamps; Garden Statuary; Sports Memorabilia; Vintage Cars; and Wine. Having seen the breadth of the salesroom's capability, it will not surprise the reader to hear of a recent successful sale of Russian space equipment, including a space suit, as has been mentioned. The auction rooms are ready to tackle any area of the market if they feel that the services offered are likely to provide a suitable means of selling. The general mode of operation is clear; if in doubt, call the auction room and ask. Sunken treasure from the Spanish fleet of 1715 sold successfully at auction. The Jacqueline Kennedy Onassis sale exemplified Sotheby's imaginative marketing skills.

As an inspection of any sales catalogue will show, the sale is put together with extreme care. Not only does the department make sure that the sale is composed of material that will be mutually complementary, but the very order in which the lots are offered has significance. A sale may contain several sessions, depending on the number of lots available for sale and the amount of items that a particular market is able to absorb at a given moment. Obviously, some of the decisions made are based on what consignments have been secured by the salesroom, but the auction rooms do much of the work of pulling together an attractive combination of lots. The length of a session is basically determined by the number of lots that can be sold at auction in a given time. This will vary according to the type of work of art being sold. A regular sale can be sold as rapidly as 2 lots a minute; in this case, a session can readily accommodate 200 lots. Since a major impressionist sale would require as much as 2 minutes per lot, a session of more than 80 lots would be inadvisable. In some cases, where there is a theme week in a particular area, a catalogue may contain as many as 1,000 lots, being sold in

morning, afternoon, and evening sessions over as many
as three days. Indeed, a major on-site sale may last a matter of weeks and contain over 5,000 lots, as did the Baden
Neues Schloss sale in 1995, in which 25,000 items were
sold in 6,000 lots over a fifteen-day period.

Within each session, the order in which items are presented has considerable relevance. Lot order is arranged
to give the sale a distinct rhythm, moving from low to
high value and back again, making sure that the potential
bidders do not become bored and listless or that all the
best items are sold together at the beginning of the sale,
allowing major bidders to leave the salesroom while the
lesser items are coming up. The look of the catalogue itself
is important; thus, the major color illustrations are evenly
spread, and each lot is given the appropriate space for
description, including subsidiary information such as
provenance, literature, exhibitions, and other important
footnotes and scholarly commentary. The description of
the Medici family birth salver in the sample catalogue
entry (pages 97–108), provides an idea of the length to
which the cataloguer may go when describing a highly
important, rare work of art.

SAMPLE CATALOGUE ENTRY

□ 69
***Giovanni di Ser Giovanni di Simone, called Lo Scheggia
(1407–1486), formerly known as the Master of the Adimari Cassone and the Master of Fucecchio**

RECTO: THE TRIUMPH OF FAME; A BIRTH SALVER (DESCO DA PARTO)
HONORING THE BIRTH OF LORENZO DE' MEDICI, IL MAGNIFICO AND
VERSO: THE MEDICI AND TORNABUONI COATS-OF-ARMS FLANKING
THE IMPRESA OF LORENZO IL MAGNIFICO

circular, tempera, silver and gold on wood in its original frame
decorated with twelve Medici feathers

*diameter: 24½ in. 62.2 cm. (painted surface); with integral frame: 36½
in. 92.7 cm.*

Given the fact the Medici coat-of-arms of eight red *palle* (balls)
within a shield and the Medici *impresa* of the three feathers with
a diamond ring appear on the verso of the present *desco da parto*
or birth tray, one of the most opulent and sophisticated to survive, its importance has long been appreciated. However, it was
only in 1905 that Aby Warburg first associated the present paint-

Portrait of Lorenzo de' Medici, School of Verrochio

ing with an entry in the 1492 inventory of the Palazzo Medici
(see literature below). On folio 14 (see E. Muntz in literature
below; there is a typescript of the inventory in the Warburg
Institute, London), half way down the page, there is listed in
Lorenzo's room "uno descho tondo daparto dipintovi iltrionfo
della fama" ("in the room of the grand hall known as Lorenzo's
. . . a circular birth tray painted with a triumph of fame"), valued
at 10 *fiorini* (200 *scudi*). The Medici coat-of-arms in the upper left
on the verso of the *tondo* is paired in the upper right with the
coat-of-arms (a rampant lion) of the Tornabuoni family. (The
twelve Medici feathers of four colors decorate the outer edge of
the painted surface on the recto.) The two coats-of-arms bring

together Lucrezia Tornabuoni and Piero de' Medici who were married in grand ceremony in 1444. The object of so important a liaison, of course, was to produce a male heir for the Medici family. And, given the subject of the tray (traditionally commissioned or acquired only on the occasion of marriages or births, and particularly popular in Tuscany) as well as the fact that the three feathers with the diamond ring and the motto *SEMPER* on a ribbon, the *impresa* of Lorenzo (only later called Il Magnifico) de' Medici, it is more than likely that the present *desco da parto* was commissioned by Piero de' Medici immediately just after the birth of his first son, Lorenzo, on January 1, 1449. (For a discussion of the Medici heraldic devices see F. Cardini in exhibited below, 1992, pp. 55–74; it is not impossible that the *impresa* may have been added later in the century; see G. Caradente in literature below). As such, the salver is without doubt the most important *desco da parto* amongst the forty or so known surviving examples, and the only one which can be associated with a specific patron and cited in a specific and contemporary inventory. *The Triumph of Fame* is next mentioned two years later as amongst the Medici possessions sold by the Sindaco of Florence when the family was expelled from Florence after Lorenzo's death in 1492. It was acquired by one Bartolomeo di Bambelo of Florence for a third of its 1492 value (see C. Däubler in literature below). The *tondo* most likely remained in Florence during the intervening two centuries; it was acquired there, possibly at auction, by the French diplomat and collector Alexis-François Artaud de Montor (1772–1849) who himself later published it in 1811 (and again in 1843, as Giotto, see literature below and note before lot 14). The birth salver was then acquired from the Artaud de Montor sale of 1851 (see provenance below) by the New Yorker Thomas Jefferson Bryan who bequeathed it to the New-York Historical Society less than twenty-five years later.

The subject of the Medici *desco da parto* is the *Triumph of Fame*, a subject of considerable interest in literature of the early Italian Renaissance. The sources of the depiction are taken quite generally from Boccaccio's *L'Amorosa visione*, specifically Book VI, of 1342 and repeated with considerable literary freedom by Francesco Petrarch in his *Trionfi* written between 1352 and 1374. Winged Fame stands with arms outstretched; in her right hand a sword and in the left a statuette of Cupid with his bow drawn.

She surmounts an articulated globe pierced by six portholes out of which six winged trumpets sound, hearalding the arrival of the newborn and his anticipated fame. Surrounding the central pedestal upon which Fame stands are knights (most in armour) on horseback each of whom with upraised right hand swears fealty to the winged goddess. Two disshevelled and barefoot figures (identified by Boccaccio as Spendius and Mathos) are

69 *recto*

visible at the bottom of the structure. Three dogs of three different colored coats fill the foreground. The compositionally formal, symmetrically balanced scene is flanked by two flowering trees and the background is made up of angular, articulated hills coming in from each side; a watery inlet flanked by two forts completes the vision behind Fame. The design of the *tondo* exemplifies the artistic rigour of one-point perspective (by mid-century, extremely popular in Florence). In addition, the *tondo* format is consciously anchored by the erect, vertical of the figure of Fame whose outstretched wings touch the edges of the compositional field and support the curved frame; it is she who keeps the circular panel from visually spinning.

The attribution of the Medici salver is now generally given to Giovanni di Ser Giovanni di Simone, called Lo Scheggia, the younger brother of Masaccio. When acquired by Artaud de

69 verso

Montor, however, it was ascribed to Giotto and it was with this attribution that Bryan bought it at the 1851 sale (see lithograph illustration). The name "Giotto" was maintained until the end of the 19th century when Berenson (see literature below, 1896) suggested Piero della Francesca as its author (later Francesco di Antonio). This suggestion at least had the advantage of moving the *tondo* into its proper chronology. Later connoisseurs suggested Domenico Veneziano who probably visited Florence in the 1440's and influenced an impressionable generation of artists; he did, after all, write a famous letter to Pietro on April 1, 1438, begging for assistance in securing work from Cosimo de'

Medici. Gradually, with greater study and photographic visibility, the *desco da parto* was associated with several anonymous Florentine artists whose eponymous works are the Adimari cassone (in the Accademia in Florence) and the Fucecchio altarpiece (near Empoli). It was R. Longhi (see literature below, 1926) who first suggested that all these various works were, in fact, by one artist. But it took almost a half century of further scholarship until a specific name could be attached to the artist of all these paintings. Luciano Bellosi finally associated the various eponymous works of art with Giovanni di Ser Giovanni (see *Mostra d'arte sacra della diocesi di San Miniato,* 1969). This, alas, does not mean, however, that there is complete agreement on this attribution. The *tondo* does indeed recall the work of Domenico Veneziano (who was, after all, in Florence for some years and therefore influenced stylistic development there; see, for example, K. Christiansen, J. Pope-Hennessy and C. Eisler in literature below) and his name has recently been invoked again (see C. Däubler in literature below).

Giovanni di Ser Giovanni, called Lo Scheggia, the brother of highly important and influential Masaccio, was born the year of his father's death and it was left to his grandfather to teach the young man. By 1420 he was a *garzone,* or apprentice, in the Bicci di Lorenzo workshop; he remained there for a little over a year and is next heard of working with his brother on the altarpiece for the Chapel of Ser Giuliano di Colino degli Scarsi in the Carmine in Pisa. By 1427 he is listed as living with his brother in the via dei Servi in Florence and in 1433 was a member of the Compagnia di San Luca. Three years later he matriculated into the Arte dei Medici e Speziali. From 1436 to 1440 he is recorded working on the *intarsia* of the cabinets in the sacristy of the Duomo; he continued to specialize in woodwork and painted furniture, especially *cassone* and *deschi da parto.* His one signed painting is in San Lorenzo in San Giovanni Valdarno (see *L'età di Masaccio; il primo Quattrocento a Firenze,* 1990, p. 256, ed. by L. Berti and A. Paolucci). It should not come as a surprise to find Piero de' Medici going to a specialist in woodwork and painted decorations for such an important commemorative object as a *desco da parto* for Lorenzo though there is no doubt that the particularly erudite subject was dictated to the painter, probably by an intellectual advisor to Piero. Piero de' Medici's love of overt opulence (especially through a heavy use of gold) to indicate taste and wealth was more than amply anticipated by Lo Scheggia. *The Triumph of Fame,* a *desco da parto* commissioned by a loving Medici father for the birth of his first son, is a masterpiece of a genre which very soon disappeared from the Medici collections after the demise of Lorenzo himself.

Provenance:
Commissioned by Piero de' Medici (1416–1469), Il Gottoso, on the occasion of the birth of his first son, Lorenzo de' Medici (later called Il Magnifico)
Lorenzo de' Medici (1449–1492), later called Il Magnifico, and listed in the 1492 inventory of the Palazzo Medici in the via Larga made after his death as being in the "sala grande" of Lorenzo himself (see Archivio di Stato Fiorentino, MAP 165, c. 14)
Bartolomeo di Bambelo, Florence, by whom bought at the sale of Medici possessions in 1494–95 (see Archivio de Stato Fiorentino, MAP 129, c. 357; see C. Däubler in literature below)
Abbé Rimani, Florence, by 1801 from whom acquired by
Alexis-François Artaud de Montor (1772–1849), Paris (His Sale: Paris, Place des Bourse, January 16–17, 1851, lot 57, as Giotto), where acquired by
Thomas Jefferson Bryan (1802–1870), New York, by whom given to the present owner in 1867 (1867.5)

Exhibited:
New York, Metropolitan Museum of Art, on loan irregularly from *circa* 1979–1993
Florence, Palazzo Medici Riccardi, *Le Tems Revient, 'L Tempo Si Rinuova, Feste e Spettacoli nella Firenze di Lorenzo Il Magnifico,* April 8–June 30, 1992, pp. 155–56, no. 2.7, illus. p. 156 (entry by Maria Sframeli)

Literature:
A.-F. Artaud de Montor, *Considérations sur l'état de la peinture en Italie,* 1811, pp. 80–82, no. 57 (as Giotto)
P. M. Gault de Saint-Germain, *Guide des Amateurs de Peinture,* 1835, pp. 53–4
A.-F. Artaud de Montor, *Peintres primitifs; Collection de tableaux rapportée d'Italie, sous la direction de M. Challamel,* 1843, pp. 34–36, no. 57, pl. 20 (as Giotto)
Bryan Catalogue, 1853, p. 1, no. 4 (as Giotto)

Bryan Companion Catalogue, 1853, pp. 6–7, no. (as Giotto)

E. Müntz, *Les Collections des Médicis au XVe siècle,* 1888, p. 63 (archival citation; see now, G. Gaeta Bertelà and M. Spallanzani, eds., *Libro d' inventario dei beni di Lorenzo Il Magnifico,* 1992, p. 27)

B. Berenson, "Les peintres italiennes de New York et de Boston," *Gazette des Beaux-Arts,* XV, 1896, p. 196 (as Piero della Francesca)

B. Berenson, *Central Italian Painters of the Renaissance,* 1897, p. 169 (as an early work by Piero della Francesca)

A. Schmarsow, "Maitres Italiens; à la galerie d'Altenburg et dans la collection A. de Montor," *Gazette des Beaux-Arts,* XX, 1898, p. 504 (as Paolo Uccello)

A. Warburg, "Della impresa amorose nelle più antiche incisione fiorentine," *Rivista d'arte,* III, 1905, p. 5 (as Florentine School)

L. Einstein and F. Monod, "Le Musée de la Société Historique de New York," *Gazette des Beaux-Arts,* May 1905, p. 416–17, illus. (as manner of Piero della Francesca)

B. Berenson, *Central Italian Painters of the Renaissance,* 1909, p. 226 (as an early(?) work by Piero della Francesca)

W. Rankin, *Rassegna d'Arte,* March 1907, p. 43 (as school of Domenico Veneziano) *Catalogue,* 1915, p. 57, no. B-5, illus. opp. p. 60 (as Giotto)

P. Schubring, *Cassoni,* 1915, vol. I, p. 272, no. 212, illus. vol. II, pl. XLIV, no. 212 (as school of Domenico Veneziano)

R. Offner, "Italian Pictures at the New York Historical Society and Elsewhere, III.," *Art in America,* VIII, 1920, pp. 8–13, fig. 3 (as Florentine School)

F. J. Mather, "Three Florentine Furniture Panels . . . ," *Art in America,* VIII, 1920, pp. 148–52, fig. 1 (as workshop of Domenico Veneziano)

F. J. Mather, *History of Italian Painting,* 1923, p. 182, illus. (as a follower of Domenico Veneziano, perhaps Baldovinetti)

R. Longhi (under the pseudonym Andrea Ronchi), "Primizie di Lorenzo da Viterbo," *Vita artistica,* I, 1926, pp. 113–14 (as Masaccio's younger brother)

H. Comstock, "Primitives from the Bryan Collection," *International Studio,* vol. LXXXIV, no. 348, May 1926, p. 30

R. van Marle, *The Development of the Italian Schools of Painting,* vol. X, 1928, p. 332 (as school of Domenico Veneziano)

R. van Marle, *The Development of the Italian Schools of Painting,* vol. XI, 1929, pp. 10–11 (as school of Domenico Veneziano)

B. Berenson, "Quadri senza casa.-Il Quattrocento fiorentino, I,"
Dedalo, XII, 1932, pp. 512–541 (as Francesco di Antonio di Banchi)
A. Warburg, *Gesammelte Schriften*, 1932, I, p. 82 (as Florentine
School)

69 detail

L. Venturi, *Italian Paintings in America*, vol. II, 1933, pl. 201 (as
school of Domenico Veneziano) D. Shorr, "Some Notes on the
Iconography of Petrarch's Triumph of Fame", *The Art Bulletin*,
XX, 1938, p. 107, fig. 6

R. Longhi, "Fatti di Masolino e di Masaccio," *Critica d'Arte*, 1940, pp. 186–87 (as possibly Lazzaro Vasari)

B. Berenson, *Italian Pictures of the Renaissance; Florentine School*, 1963, vol. I, p. 63; vol. II, no. 732, illus. (as Francesco di Antonio di Banchi on a design by Domenico Veneziano)

lithograph from Peintres primitifs, *plate 20*

G. Caradente, *I Trionfi del primo Rinascimento*, 1963, p. 305, note 132

G. Previtali, *La Fortuna dei Primitivi dal Vasari ai Neoclassici*, 1964, p. 178

B. Berenson, *Homeless Paintings of the Renaissance*, 1969, pp. 165–68 (as Francesco di Antonio)

B. Fredericksen and F. Zeri, *Census of Pre-Nineteenth Century Italian Paintings in North American Public Collections*, 1972, pp. 129, 609 (as Master of Fucecchio)

R. Fremantle, *Florentine Gothic Painters*, 1975, p. 642 (as Master of Fucecchio)

69 detail

H. Wohl, *The Paintings of Domenico Veneziano*, 1980, pp. 165–66, no. 37, illus. 201–202 (as Giovanni di Ser Giovanni)

J. Pope-Hennessy and K. Christiansen, "Secular Painting in 15th-Century Tuscany: Birth Trays, Cassone Panels, and Portraits," *Metropolitan Museum of Art Bulletin*, XXXVIII, Summer 1980, pp. 9, 11, illus. in color (as Giovanni di Ser Giovanni)

D. C. Ahl, "Renaissance Birth Salvers and the Richmond *Judgment of Solomon*," *Studies in Iconography*, 7–8, 1981–82, pp. 157–74, esp. pp. 160–61, note 35, illus. 7 (as Giovanni di Ser Giovanni)

C. Eisler, "A Window on Domenico Veneziano at Santa Croce," in *Scritti di storia dell'arte in onore di Federico Zeri*, 1984, pp. 130–33, esp. p. 131 (as close to Domenico Veneziano)

G. Previtali, *La Fortuna dei Primitivi dal Vasari ai Neoclassici*, 1989, p. 178

C. Däubler, *Deschi e Tazze da Parto: Presents for Women in Childbed in the Italian Renaissance*, Ph.D Diss., Augsburg University, Augsburg, in course of completion (as close to Domenico Veneziano)

Clearly, the average lot receives less attention than this rare masterpiece, but it is important that the potential buyer be made aware of the relevant facts. At a minimum, a catalogue description must give the artist, the craftsman or maker, where known, the place of origin, the date, a verbal description, all identifying marks, the measurements, provenance, exhibitions, and literature, where known, so that the item can be positively identified and distinguished from all other similar items. In these days, the vast majority of lots are also illustrated either in color or black and white. A word of caution is in order as far as color illustrations are concerned. It is notoriously difficult to create accurate color illustrations, and the buyer is strongly encouraged to inspect every item in person, a good habit from many points of view. Footnotes and other additional information should be read with due care, for it is here that the specialist can fill out the surrounding facts that can establish the true importance of a work of art. The buyer should take advantage of this knowledge in deciding whether or not to bid.

The catalogue contains other important information. Regardless of whether the information is found at the front or the back of the catalogue, it is worth careful study. The dates and times of the public exhibition appear on the title page together with the sale number and code name for the sale. This information is important if the prospective buyer plans to visit the exhibition and then to leave a written bid with the galleries. There follows a listing of various gallery employees who may be consulted in the process. The roles are self-explanatory but give a good sense of the breadth of services offered by the auction house. Client Advisory Services list representatives who will inspect items for a client, offer advice not always available in the catalogue, and execute bids on behalf of clients. These agents usually form a long-term relationship with their clients and can be enormously useful in a number of ways, acting somewhat like a personal banking representative. Also listed are those who deal exclusively with absentee bids, payment, and shipping, and those who are directly responsible for these activities as they relate to a particular sale. The experts in charge of a sale from the specialist department or departments are also listed so that a client is able to call one who will know the sale in every detail and who can, once again, supply much information that cannot be put in the catalogue. This information might include a discussion of the thinking that lay behind the estimate and a review of similar pieces sold in the recent past as well as a detailed statement on condition.

There follows a lengthy section entitled "Conditions of Sale." This is the small print. I do not believe that it is necessary to read this section every time one attends an auction and am willing to bet that no client does so. However, these conditions do change from time to time, and I do recommend that a client read them on a regular basis, at least at the beginning of each auction season. The auctioneer reminds those present at every auction of these conditions. One who has never bid at auction before is strongly encouraged to do his or her homework.

The "Terms of Guarantee" that follow are, again, important statements concerning the auction house's warranties and guarantees. These are perhaps even more essential reading for the potential bidder than the "Conditions of Sale" since they explain what the various terms used in the catalogue mean, most especially in terms of authorship and authenticity. The lawyers have clearly had a field day, but this does not negate the importance of their work, whereby the buyer is placed in full knowledge of the conditions under which bidding is conducted. These conditions and terms might be compared to a patient's "Bill of Rights" in a hospital, although we trust that the auction experience will prove more pleasurable.

The next section of the catalogue offers a "Guide for Prospective Sellers" and a "Guide for Prospective Buyers" (see pages 110 and 114). These two sections are sufficiently succinct and useful that I have reproduced them in full since they offer essential information to both constituencies.

GUIDE FOR PROSPECTIVE SELLERS

Conservation Law. Although licenses can be obtained to export some items which are the subject of these laws, other items may not be exported (such as items containing whale bone), and some property may not be resold in the United States. Upon request, Sotheby's is willing to assist a purchaser in attempting to obtain appropriate licenses. However, there is no assurance that an export license can be obtained. Sotheby's will charge a minimum fee of $150 per item if it is able to obtain an export license. Please check with the specialist department or with the Art Transport Department if you are uncertain as to whether an item is affected by the above laws or other related laws which restrict exportation. The sale of a purchased lot will not be cancelled if Sotheby's, or a purchaser, is not able to obtain an export permit.

PROPERTY OWNED BY SOTHEBY'S

In the event Sotheby's is the sole owner of any lot in an auction, Sotheby's ownership will be designated either by a symbol, or in a manner such as the following: "Property of Sotheby's", or "Property from the Estate of Mrs. Smith, sold by the present owner, Sotheby's."

Where Sotheby's has an equity interest in property other than sole ownership, that interest will be designated by the symbol, △.

As an example:

△ Pierre-Auguste Renoir

☐ 22   Femme au Corsage Bleu

GUARANTEED PROPERTY

Guaranteed Property is property in which Sotheby's has assured the seller a minimum price from one auction, or a series of auctions. Guaranteed property will be designated in the catalogue by the symbol, ○. Where every lot in a catalogue is guaranteed, Sotheby's will not designate each lot with the symbol, ○, but will state in boldface type on the Conditions of Sale page that every lot in the sale is subject to a guaranteed minimum price.

If you have property you wish to sell at auction, please call the appropriate specialist department to arrange for a consultation. (A list of specialist departments appears in the front of this catalogue.) If you are unsure which department would handle your property, or if you have a variety of objects to sell, please call one of our general representatives:

Fine Arts Representative
Thomas Denzler, (212) 606-7120

Decorative Arts Representative
Timothy Hamilton, (212) 606-7100

INSPECTION OF PROPERTY

You may bring your property, or photographs if it is not portable, directly to our galleries where our specialists will give you auction estimates and advice. There is no charge for this service, but we request that you telephone ahead for an appointment. Inspection hours are 9:30 am to 5 pm, Monday through Friday.

Our specialists will provide a free preliminary auction estimate, subject to a final auction estimate after first-hand inspection, if you send a clear photograph of each item, or a representative group of photographs if you have a large collection. Please be sure to include the dimensions, artist's signature or maker's mark, medium, physical condition, and any other relevant information.

Evaluations of property can also be made at your home. The fees for such visits are based on the scope and diversity of the collection. Travel expenses are additional. These fees may be rebated if you consign your property for sale at Sotheby's.

Specialists from our Beverly Hills office are available for inspection visits in the western United States. For more information please call (310) 274-0340.

STANDARD COMMISSION RATES

Sellers are charged 10% of the successful bid price for each lot sold for $7,500 or more. A commission of 15% is charged for each lot sold for $2,000 or more but less than $7,500, and 20% for each lot sold for less than $2,000. There is a minimum handling charge of $100 for any lot sold. If your property fails to reach the reserve price and remains unsold, you pay a reduced commission rate of 5% of the reserve figure. The minimum handling charge for any object that does not sell is $75. (For more information about reserves, please refer to "Reserves" in "Guide to Prospective Buyers.")

SHIPPING ARRANGEMENTS

Sotheby's Art Transport Department and the staff at any of our regional offices can assist you in making arrangements to have your property delivered to our galleries. This service is free, but actual packing, shipping and insurance charges are payable by our clients. (While we may recommend packers and shippers, we are not responsible for their acts or omissions.) For further information, please call Leslie Kirkman at (212) 606-7511.

APPRAISALS

Sotheby's Appraisal Company can prepare appraisals for insurance, estate tax, charitable contributions, family division or other purposes.

Appraisal fees vary according to the nature and amount of work to be undertaken, but will always be highly competitive. Flat rates can be quoted based on specialist time required, value and processing costs. Travel expenses are additional.

We shall be pleased to refund the appraisal fee pro rata if the appraised property is consigned to us for sale within one year after the appraisal is completed. For further information please call (212) 606-7440.

FINANCIAL SERVICES

Sotheby's offers a wide range of financial services. These financial services include advances on consignments and loans secured by art collections which are not intended for sale. It is Sotheby's general policy, subject to exceptions, to lend no more than 40% of the total of its low estimates for such property. It is also Sotheby's general policy, subject to exceptions, that the minimum loan for consignor advances is $50,000, and the minimum loan for secured loans is $1,000,000. For further information regarding qualifications, conditions, and terms, please call Mitchell Zuckerman at (212) 606-7077.

CATALOGUES, PRICE LISTS AND NEWSLETTER

Illustrated catalogues, prepared by Sotheby's specialists, are published for all regularly scheduled auctions and may be purchased singly or by annual subscription. (Catalogue subscribers automatically receive *At Sotheby's* at no additional charge.)

Printed lists of the prices realized at each auction are available at our galleries approximately three weeks following the auction, and are sent directly to catalogue purchasers and subscribers.

At Sotheby's, published seven times a year, provides an advance calendar of all Sotheby's sales worldwide and full-color photographs of auction highlights. A complimentary copy is available upon request. Annual subscriptions are $25 ($35 overseas).

For more information, or to subscribe to our catalogues or *At Sotheby's,* ask for our brochure. Write or call Sotheby's Subscription Department, P.O. Box 5111, Norwalk, CT 06856. Telephone: 1-800-444-3709.

GUIDE FOR PROSPECTIVE BUYERS

The following will help explain some of the words and symbols commonly used throughout this catalogue. All bidders should read the Conditions of Sale and Terms of Guarantee in this catalogue, as well as any Glossary or other notices. By bidding at auction, bidders are bound by those Conditions of Sale and Terms of Guarantee, as amended by any oral announcement or posted notices, which together form the contract of sale between the successful bidder (purchaser), Sotheby's and the seller (consignor) of the lot. Please remember that all property is sold "As Is" and is only subject to rescission as stated in any applicable Terms of Guarantee. If you have any questions concerning the information below or any other auction practices, please contact Roberta Louckx at 606-7414.

ESTIMATES

Each lot in the catalogue is given a low and high estimate. The estimates are guides for prospective bidders and, where possible, reflect prices that similar objects have sold for in the past. The estimates are determined several months before a sale and are therefore subject to revision to reflect current market conditions. Estimates should not be relied upon as a representation or prediction of actual selling prices. If you have any questions concerning a lot, please contact the specialist in charge of the sale whose name is printed in the front of this catalogue.

SPECIALIST ADVICE; EXHIBITIONS

Prospective bidders may be interested in specific information which is not included in the catalogue description of a lot. Do not hesitate to contact Sotheby's specialist in charge listed in the front of the catalogue, or Sotheby's Client Services Department, for additional information. A few days prior to every sale, there will be an exhibition of the property to be offered. Specialists will be available at the exhibition to answer questions about the property or to provide any other assistance with the auction process. The dates and times of the exhibition are printed in the front of this catalogue.

BIDDING

In order to bid at an auction, you must register for a paddle when entering the salesroom. If you are the successful bidder on a lot, the auctioneer will acknowledge your paddle number. Unless you have previously qualified to bid at Sotheby's, please be prepared to provide requested information to a Sotheby's representative.

Bidding will be in accordance with the lot numbers listed in the catalogue or as announced by the auctioneer, and will be in increments determined by the auctioneer. There are three ways in which you may bid at auction. You may bid in person by attending the auction, submit an Absentee Bid Form, or in certain circumstances, by telephone. If you are unable to attend the sale, please see the Absentee Bid Form and Guide for Absentee Bidders which contains additional information on absentee bidding.

Unless otherwise noted in the catalogue or by an announcement at the auction, Sotheby's acts as agent on behalf of the seller and does not permit the seller to bid on his or her own property. It is important for all bidders to know that the auctioneer may open the bidding on any lot by placing a bid on behalf of the seller and may continue bidding for the seller by placing responsive or consecutive bids, but only up to the reserve (see the next paragraph below for information regarding reserves). The auctioneer will not place consecutive bids on behalf of the seller above the reserve.

RESERVES

All property designated by a box (□) is offered subject to a reserve. A reserve is the confidential minimum price established between Sotheby's and the seller. The reserve is generally set at a percentage of the low estimate and will not exceed the low estimate of the lot.

CURRENCY CONVERSION BOARD

For your convenience, in many sales Sotheby's operates a display board which converts United States dollars into various foreign currencies. All foreign currency amounts displayed are approximations based on recent exchange rate information and may not be relied upon as a precise invoice amount. Sotheby's assumes no responsibility for any error or omission in foreign or United States currency amounts shown.

HAMMER PRICE (OR SUCCESSFUL BID PRICE) AND THE BUYER'S PREMIUM

For lots which are sold, the last price for a lot as announced by the auctioneer is the hammer, or successful bid price. A buyer's premium will be added to the successful bid price and is payable by the purchaser as part of the total purchase price. The buyer's premium will be the amount stated in Paragraph 3 of the Conditions of Sale in the front of this catalogue.

PAYMENT FOR PURCHASED PROPERTY

If you are the successful bidder on a lot, payment is to be made immediately following a sale. You will not be permitted to take delivery of your purchases until payment is made, unless a credit arrangement has been established. Please contact the specialist in charge of the sale, or Arlene Kick at (212) 606-7491, for information on a specific lot.

Payment for a lot may be made in United States dollars by cash, check, or coin transfer. Payment may also be made by American Express, Visa or MasterCard, subject to the following conditions.

Payment by Charge or Credit Card
If you wish to pay for any purchase with your American Express Card, MasterCard or Visa, you must present the card *in person* to Sotheby's at the auction, or within five days of the auction. If

you do not plan to be present at the auction, and wish to pay with the American Express Card, please come to Sotheby's in advance of the auction, present the card in person and complete an Advance Form (available at the Purchaser Accounting Desk). If your bid is successful, within five days of the auction you will need to sign and return to Sotheby's a confirming purchaser invoice (which will be provided to you by Sotheby's). All charges are subject to acceptance by Sotheby's and by American Express, MasterCard or Visa, as the case may be. In the case a charge is not approved, you will nevertheless be liable to Sotheby's for all sums incurred by you.

Payment by check

If you wish to pay by check, please see our cashier and fill out a Check Acceptance Account form. Until approved, you will not be permitted to remove purchases paid for by check until the check has cleared. Check Acceptance privileges are reviewed from time to time by Sotheby's, and may be granted or withdrawn in Sotheby's sole discretion. Checks drawn on foreign banks may not be accepted for values under $500, and credit card purchases may not exceed $25,000. There will be a collection charge minimum of $100 on checks drawn on foreign banks located outside of the continental United States.

SALES TAX

New York sales tax is charged on the successful bid price, buyer's premium and any other applicable charges on any property picked up or delivered in New York State, regardless of the state or country in which the purchaser resides or does business, unless Sotheby's has been given, in advance of the release of the property, a valid exemption from taxes by the State of New York. Sotheby's will also collect taxes on purchases shipped to California, Connecticut, Florida, Illinois, Massachusetts, Minnesota, New Jersey, Pennsylvania and Washington, D.C. If you have any questions concerning this, please contact our Customer Billing Department at (212) 606-7464.

REMOVAL OF PROPERTY; PACKING AND SHIPPING

Unless otherwise agreed by Sotheby's, all purchases should be removed by the 10th day following a sale. Purchases which are not removed by the 10th day will be subject to a handling charge as outlined in paragraph 8 of the Conditions of Sale.

As a courtesy to purchasers who come to Sotheby's to pick up property, Sotheby's will assist in the packing of lots, although Sotheby's may, in the case of fragile articles, choose not to pack or otherwise handle a purchase. Sotheby's will not be responsible or liable for damage to glass covering paintings, drawings or other works, or damage to frames, regardless of the cause.

Sotheby's Art Transport Department and the staff at Sotheby's regional offices may be able to assist you in making arrangements for delivery and insuring of purchases. The purchaser will be responsible for shipping and insurance expenses. Sotheby's will also, upon request, provide names of professional packers and shippers known to the Art Transport Department, although Sotheby's shall have no liability or responsibility for providing this information. If you have any questions or wish further information, please contact the Art Transport Department at (212) 606-7511.

EXPORT PERMITS

Certain property sold at auction may be subject to the provisions of the Endangered Species Act of 1973, the Marine Mammal Protection Act of 1972, the Migratory Bird Act of 1982 and the New York State Environmental Conservation Law.

Some of these areas of concern will be dealt with in greater detail in later sections of this book, but the broad introduction offered provides a good overview of the process at hand. Given that commission rates are subject to change, these rates are only offered as a broad guideline. The interested party is advised to call the auction house prior to any transaction in order to confirm the current applicable rates.

Following the guides to selling and buying, a glossary is often included, explaining the terms of art used in a particular area. This glossary may also be found on occasion at the end of the catalogue. In areas such as prints, this section will be useful in defining editions or states of prints, medium, date, condition, and so forth. It goes without saying that such information helps to establish better understanding of what the catalogue is telling the potential buyer.

The catalogue is an invaluable tool for collectors, whether they intend to bid in a particular sale or not. Coupled with the price lists that are published following each sale, the catalogue provides an immediate review of the current market together with price levels and access to scholarship in a given field. The collector will usually subscribe to a series of catalogues annually, covering those areas of expertise that affect the collection in question. The study of back catalogues can prove a useful introduction to a field of collecting, identifying trends and giving a picture of the availability of works of art in the category of interest. Much of this information is now available on computer, but there is no substitute for the exercise of looking through the catalogue and associating a price with a particular illustrated lot. The knowledge gained is only surpassed by being present in the salesroom and absorbing the prices as they are created in the auction process itself.

Marketing and Promotion

It has been suggested that a good work of art could be offered at the North Pole at midnight and the interested dealers and collectors would show up, such is the efficiency of the "bush telegraph" in the art world. But the major auction houses spend much time and money in promoting and marketing their sales. In the past twenty years, most markets in the arts have become truly international. This has led to a significant growth in the value of works of art while necessitating much greater efforts in the areas of marketing and promotion. Advertisement in the appropriate art magazines and journals, in the local newspapers, and in other organs dedicated to specialized fields are among the essential elements of a successful sale. Large press offices in the major auction centers are actively engaged in getting the stories out to the media, with press releases flowing daily to announce upcoming sales and to analyze results for the media, always looking for the human side of the auction story. The "trophy" sales of the estates of famous persons attract huge media attention, as witnessed by the sale of Andy Warhol's, Rudolf Nureyev's, and Jackie Onassis's properties. Auction houses understand that public recognition is an essential element of their success and, therefore, compete furiously for the big-name properties, sometimes risking profitability in order to prevent a great name from landing in the opposition's schedule of sales.

The marketing departments of the major houses are constantly developing new methods of gaining an edge in this competition. Lectures, symposia, study courses, and other educational opportunities abound. Heirloom Discovery Days, in which items are orally appraised for a small fee donated to a museum or other institution, have become a common fixture. Auction Adventures, in which groups are taught the basics of buying and selling at a mock auction, have proved popular, removing the mystery from the process and encouraging new potential buyers to make the first bold step through the doors of the big auction houses. Private views and gallery walks aid in bringing individual sales exhibitions to the attention of interested parties. Benefit views and charity auctions introduce an ever-increasing public to the advantages of the auction method. All these initiatives are designed to make the potential bidder feel familiar and comfortable with the process. Thus prepared by an examination of the catalogue and forewarned of the opportunity by the efforts of the Marketing and Public Relations Department, the potential bidder is now ready to attend a sales exhibition, the beginning of the actual sales process itself.

Viewing the Exhibition: Active Browsing

Auction houses invest considerable time, money, and effort in presenting items for sale in an attractive surrounding. There is, after all, less than a week of public view in which it is hoped that a prospective buyer will fall in love with every item on display. Exhibitions are put together in a manner that suggests the interior of a home and, at the same time, invites the would-be purchaser to inspect the works of art with total thoroughness. The client is actively encouraged to touch, handle, examine, and ask questions about any item that is of interest. Small or fragile items are displayed in cases, but this does not prevent the customer from requesting the opening of the case by a salesroom attendant. The auction house understands that client satisfaction is much more likely when the inspection process has been easy and thorough. Since I have been viewing sales exhibitions for over thirty years, I am happy to confess my own system, which guarantees that all the ground has been covered and no hidden discovery overlooked. First, walk over the entire exhibition area, starting on the left wall next to the door and continuing clockwise around the room on the outside wall. Next circle any cases, also in a clockwise direction. Where the exhibition is in an open area, create your own "room" definitions. As you proceed on your first cursory inspection, note the items that particularly draw your attention, marking their lot numbers and locations in your sales catalogue (for example, "South Gallery, west wall" or "Third-floor gallery, center showcase"). This will remove your anxiety at the possibility of getting stuck looking at one item when there might be a better one in the next room or of running out of time and not getting around to the whole sale. Having taken the broad overview, when you return to look at a particular item in detail, you will find your ability to concentrate on that item greatly enhanced.

Having established the shortlist of items that attracted your attention, you now return and concentrate totally on the particular item. First, look at it generally. What is it about this work that attracts you? To be mildly anthropomorphic, are you *really* in love with the object at hand? If the answer is yes, you must now become totally objective, asking the same questions that the expert cataloguer has asked. Is it the right age? What condition is it in? Have there been any alterations or restorations? Who created it? When? If it is signed, inscribed, or dated, are these indicators genuine or the work of an unscrupulous later hand? How does this subject fit into the artist's or craftsman's oeuvre? Does the catalogue make any references to provenance, exhibitions, or scholarly literature?

Assuming that the love affair continues after this cold-blooded appraisal, the viewer should now test the object as to value. What will this bring at sale? Does the printed estimate in the catalogue seem low, high, or right on target? Does this fit within the potential buyer's "comfort range"? Is it of the very best quality within its field? Here, the collector reviews the ten criteria of quality, which we have already examined. I believe that the intelligent collector does all of this before moving to the next stage—that of consulting the resident expert—not necessarily because that expert's knowledge will be superior to that of the sophisticated collector, but because the specialist who catalogues a lot may have access to information that the potential buyer does not have and that could not, for any number of reasons, be included in the catalogue. Questions about condition and quality are appropriate. The potential buyer might like to ask the expert to compare an item with similar items either in the current sale or from past sales. It is expected that a departmental specialist be willing to give an explanation for a particular estimate. Specialists are also willing to respond to inquiries concerning the amount of interest that has or has not been shown in an item during an exhibition, though the specialist cannot divulge the names of those who have shown interest any more than your name will be given out. Specialists love to talk about items in their sales, and they know that the best advice they can give you is the truth because then you will come back for more. One of the best pieces of advice that a specialist can give a potential buyer is what *not* to buy. It is always worth waiting for the best example and not compromising in the matter of quality.

In addition to the departmental specialists, who will be available at most times during the exhibition of a sale in their area of expertise, client service representatives are available to offer advice or execute bids on a client's behalf. Any advice they offer will have been secured from the specialist departments or from professional consultants, as in the case of restoration issues. Many clients get to know a particular client service representative and work regularly through him or her for all their needs, very much the way that some people do their banking through a personal banker. Such relationships undoubtedly take some of the anxiety and hassle out of dealing with a major auction room, but I would emphasize the importance of a collector coming to know the departmental specialists as well as possible since their knowledge is invaluable.

Having weighed the specialist's advice against your own judgment, there are then some options available, should you decide to bid, and these will be explained in Chapter III. As can be gathered, the viewing of an auction sale can be time-consuming and complex. The serious collector will, nevertheless, realize that the investment of such time and energy at this stage of the process is the ultimate key to success. If you are not prepared to make this investment, you must either buy the time and knowledge of another, such as a competent dealer, or consider staying away from this wonderful, yet complicated, market.

II

How to Sell at Auction

Choosing the Auction House

The two principal auction houses, Sotheby's and Christie's, have both been in business since the eighteenth century. Both houses have a well-established reputation. Although Christie's can truthfully claim that it is the oldest "fine art" auction house, Sotheby's, founded in 1744, has been around twenty-two years longer than its rival. Neither fact would strike me as compelling when attempting to decide between the two houses at the end of the twentieth century. How, then, is the decision to be made?

Prior to deciding between the houses, there is an important conclusion to be reached for the seller. Is auction the best approach to sale? This question can be answered by other, multiple questions: Is the work of art or the group of works attractive, in good condition, within an area that is broadly collected, in a market that is stable or strong? Has the property been off the market for a considerable period of time? If the answer to any of these questions is no, then auction may not be the best way to go. Items that have a narrow field of collection or that have recently appeared at sale or that do not generally appear at auction are at risk in this method of sale. There are occasions when either outright sale to a dealer or sale through consignment to a dealer may be the preferred route, allowing for a longer period in which to identify the appropriate buyer and leaning on a dealer's particular connections in a market that lacks a large number of collectors or buyers. Such markets are described as thin, and the risk of selling at auction may be considerable.

Where the work of art has unchallenged quality, is attractive to a broad group of collectors, and comes fresh to the market, the great advantage to the seller at auction is that the seller shares in the upside potential of the sale, understanding that fine works of art are in no way limited as to price level by their presale estimates. A dealer, understandably, makes the greatest profit by buying low and selling high. The auction house shares the success with the seller, earning a greater commission from a higher price, but always in a preset proportion that benefits the seller at the same time. The constant bombardment by the media of new auction records for works of art is testimony to the fact that, at the top of the market, new price levels are achieved at auction, which, indeed, should remain the case if the value of art is to keep pace with the value of the dollar and the cost of living.

While the media keep the world aware of the highest prices, it is worth recalling that even the major auction houses stay in business by selling a huge quantity of less valuable items. Owners of attractive but reasonable property should not be intimidated by the million-dollar hype. The auction houses want this business and will sell it efficiently and at a reasonable cost to the seller. Having said that, I should also mention that I do not believe in using an elephant to crack a nut. If a property contains little of quality, it may well sell to greater advantage at a smaller, less prestigious auction room, where it will not be compared to the goods upstairs. The major rooms will be happy to make recommendations for local reliable secondary auction rooms.

Let us assume, however, that you, the seller, have a major property, highly suitable for presentation at either

Sotheby's or Christie's at one or more of their major international auction centers. How are you going to proceed, while negotiating the best deal?

The competition between the two houses for major consignments is intense, which leaves the seller in the position of being able to structure a highly advantageous deal. Due to the need for both houses not only to carry their overheads, but also to make a reasonable profit, the seller now will pay a selling commission on a fixed scale based on the value of the consignment. This commission is no longer negotiable. Both houses will also need to recover some of the costs of placing works at auction, such as shipping, insurance, advertising, promotion, and marketing. In this area, there will be some room for negotiation, but only in the case of property with extreme value. In the normal run of business, a client can expect to make a contribution to these costs. Selling property in conjunction with other star properties can have an advantage in raising the level of interest, provided that the properties do not vie through duplication of similar major pieces. The auction houses regularly use major secured consignments to leverage further consignments, a perfectly legitimate use of advantageous circumstances. Lesser property may, however, be damaged by appearance at the same time as a stellar property in that some markets cannot absorb huge quantities of material at one time.

The market in fine American furniture is instructive in this regard. In this particular market, as in many, there is broad interest at the middle price levels, with a large number of buyers prepared to spend up to about $20,000 per item. Once the $100,000 mark is reached, the field thins out substantially, with a handful of collectors prepared to buy only the very highest quality. The principal American furniture sales traditionally take place in New York in January, timed to coincide with the Winter Antiques Show at the Armory. Thus, both the major auction houses and the top dealers are making available at the same time the highlights of their offerings in this area. If a dealer sells a Philadelphia tea table for $2 million at the preview to the Antiques Show, that $2 million is no longer available as a bid on the Goddard-Townsend kneehole desk at Sotheby's or the Duncan Phyfe worktable at Christie's. Should either house be presenting an extraordinary group during this period, the collectors may hold off making a major purchase at the Antiques Show. The experts at the auction rooms should be consulted during the consignment process in order to ascertain the existence of a competitive property either at their own house or with the competition.

On a major consignment, the seller can expect to receive a proposal from the auction house, outlining the details of the sale together with a marketing plan and a detailed listing of the property, including a low and high estimate on each item. The auction house will list its credentials in the areas of expertise involved along with a history of its past activity in that area. Copies of previous catalogues and publications will be annexed, as well as the résumés of the specialists and officers involved in the potential sale. The in-depth expertise of the auction-house employees should carry more weight than statements about market share, which, while interesting, do not necessarily convey current ability to do the best job for the client. Given the fact that commissions and costs will likely be similar, a decision to sell with one house rather than the other may rest on two principal considerations: the imaginativeness and appropriateness of the marketing plan, and the relationship established with the individual specialists and officers involved. I have on occasion, in presenting a sales proposal to a group of executors and knowing that I was in competition with the other house, stated directly to the executors that both houses will do a competent job, the estimates will be similar, the terms close if not identical, so that the decision to go with a particular house must be made on the basis of which group of people will make them feel more comfortable since the selling process involves working very closely with a client. It is on such personal considerations that major collections swing in one direction or another. I believe that this is one of the pleasant aspects of the auction business: there is room for the personal relationship; people still count.

The Initial Inquiry

The would-be seller needs to remember that there is no substitute for examining the work of art itself. Therefore, in considering a potential sale, the sooner the specialist and the object can come together, the more accurate the information is likely to be. Many decisions to sell are made on the basis of a provisional sales estimate. This estimate will be accurate only if the item for sale has been carefully examined. There is an obvious choice to be made between bringing the work of art to the expert or bringing the expert to the work of art. In many cases, it is best to reduce the movement—and, thus, the risk—to a minimum, and larger works of art are best viewed on site, especially if there are many of them. Jewelry is an obvious exception. Not only is jewelry easily transported, but the expert in this area needs the equipment in his or her office in order to make an accurate evaluation of the individual pieces. In the case of paintings, furniture, and other bulky objects, a clear photograph accompanying an original request for an estimate will prove useful to the specialist, who can then do some initial research into the item before its actual inspection. Photographs should be of reasonable size, in focus, and clearly marked with the owner's name, the size of the item, and statements as to artist, craftsman, or creator, together with any facts concerning signature, date, or other identifying marks. A multiple group of photographs should be accompanied by a checklist, each photograph numbered, so that the auction room can make sure that every item has been considered by the appropriate specialist in a multiple group of departments. It should be stressed that any estimates or comments made on the basis of photographs are extremely provisional but will at least help a potential consignor to decide whether or not a site visit is desirable.

Whether the initial contact is made through a telephone call, a letter, or a visit either to the auction house or to the client's residence, the client should remember that such contact does not commit the client to any further action and is usually conducted at no cost to the client. Given the vast geographical areas that the specialists must cover, a client should be prepared to wait for as much as four weeks to receive a visit, although in many cases a visit will take place more quickly. An initial letter of inquiry with photographs has the advantage of obtaining a response within a week or so, thereby getting the process started in a minimum of time. If the seller has a clear idea of the specialist department involved, a telephone call to the head of that department can be a good initial contact in that it is this specialist who will eventually orchestrate the details of a consignment. Once again, personal contact is the key to client satisfaction. In the case of a potentially diverse consignment, auction houses have departments specifically designed to deal with the multiple contacts required by such properties. Executives will provide liaison between the consignor and the various departments, guiding the client through the maze of documents and communications that are necessary to the process. Sellers should not feel daunted by their approach to the major houses, remembering that their business is important and provides the income that allows the auction houses to be around for the spectacular "trophy sales," when they occur.

The Terms and Conditions

The "Conditions of Sale" and the 'Terms of Guarantee" (pages 130 and 134, respectively) are given in each sales catalogue. A responsible seller should be aware of the terms under which the auction house is offering property for sale on his or her behalf. These terms and conditions are, therefore, reproduced here for the reader's use. Much of this material reads like the "boilerplate" it is. But terms and conditions do change, and the client should be aware of such changes.

CONDITIONS OF SALE

The following Conditions of Sale and Terms of Guarantee are Sotheby's, Inc. and the Consignor's entire agreement with the purchaser relative to the property listed in this catalogue. The Conditions of Sale, Terms of Guarantee, the glossary, if any, and all other contents of this catalogue are subject to amendment by us by the posting of notices or by oral announcements made during the sale. The property will be offered by us as agent for the Consignor, unless the catalogue indicates otherwise. By participating in any sale, you acknowledge that you are bound by these terms and conditions.

1.   Goods auctioned are often of some age. The authenticity of the Authorship of property listed in the catalogue is guaranteed as stated in the Terms of Guarantee and except for the Limited Warranty contained therein, all property is sold "AS IS" without any representations or warranties by us or the Consignor as to merchantability, fitness for a particular purpose, the correctness of the catalogue or other description of the physical condition, size, quality, rarity, importance, medium, provenance, exhibitions, literature or historical relevance of any property and no statement anywhere, whether oral or written, whether made in the catalogue, an advertisement, a bill of sale, a salesroom posting or announcement, or elsewhere, shall be deemed such a

warranty, representation or assumption of liability. We and the Consignor make no representations and warranties, express or implied, as to whether the purchaser acquires any copyrights, including but not limited to, any reproduction rights in any property. We and the Consignor are not responsible for errors and omissions in the catalogue, glossary, or any supplemental material.

2.   Prospective bidders should inspect the property before bidding to determine its condition, size, and whether or not it has been repaired or restored.

3.   A buyer's premium will be added to the successful bid price and is payable by the purchaser as part of the total purchase price. The buyer's premium is 15% of the successful bid price up to and including $50,000, and 10% on any amount in excess of $50,000.

4.   We reserve the right to withdraw any property before the sale and shall have no liability whatsoever for such withdrawal.

5.   Unless otherwise announced by the auctioneer, all bids are per lot as numbered in the catalogue.

6.   We reserve the right to reject any bid. The highest bidder acknowledged by the auctioneer will be the purchaser. In the event of any dispute between bidders, or in the event of doubt on our part as to the validity of any bid, the auctioneer will have the final discretion to determine the successful bidder, cancel the sale, or to reoffer and resell the article in dispute. If any dispute arises after the sale, our sale record is conclusive. Although in our discretion we will execute order or absentee bids or accept telephone bids as a convenience to clients who are not present at auctions, we are not responsible for any errors or omissions in connection therewith.

7.   If the auctioneer decides that any opening bid is below the reserve of the article offered, he may reject the same and withdraw the article from sale, and if, having acknowledged an opening bid, he decides that any advance thereafter is insufficient, he may reject the advance.

8.   Subject to fulfillment of all of the conditions set forth herein, on the fall of the auctioneer's hammer, title to the offered lot will pass to the highest bidder acknowledged by the auctioneer, and

such bidder thereupon (a) assumes full risk and responsibility therefor, and (b) will immediately pay the full purchase price or such part as we may require. In addition to other remedies available to us by law, we reserve the right to impose from the date of sale a late charge of 1½% per month of the total purchase price if payment is not made in accordance with the conditions set forth herein. All property must be removed from our premises by the purchaser at his expense not later than 10 business days following its sale and, if it is not so removed, (i) a handling charge of 1% of the total purchase price per month from the tenth day after the sale until its removal will be payable to us by the purchaser, with a minimum of 5% of the total purchase price for any property not so removed within 60 days after the sale, and (ii) we may send the purchased property to a public warehouse for the account, risk and expense of the purchaser.

If any applicable conditions herein are not complied with by the purchaser, the purchaser will be in default and in addition to any and all other remedies available to us and the Consignor by law, including without limitation the right to hold the purchaser liable for the total purchase price, including all fees, charges and expenses more fully set forth herein, we, at our option, may (x) cancel the sale of that, or any other lot or lots sold to the defaulting purchaser at the same or any other auction, retaining as liquidated damages all payments made by the purchaser, or (y) resell the purchased property, whether at public auction or by private sale, or (z) effect any combination thereof. In any case, the purchaser will be liable for any deficiency, any and all costs, handling charges, late charges, expenses of both sales, our commissions on both sales at our regular rates, legal fees and expenses, collection fees and incidental damages. We may, in our sole discretion, apply any proceeds of sale then due or thereafter becoming due to the purchaser from us or any affiliated company, or any payment made by the purchaser to us or any affiliated company, whether or not intended to reduce the purchaser's obligations with respect to the unpaid lot or lots, to the deficiency and any other amounts due to us or any affiliated companies. In addition, a defaulting purchaser will be deemed to have granted and assigned to us and our affiliated companies, a continuing security interest of first priority in any property or money of or owing to such purchaser in our possession or in the possession of any of our affiliated companies, and we may retain and apply such property or money as collateral security for the obligations due to us or to any affiliated company of ours. We shall have all of the rights accorded a secured party under the New York Uniform Commercial Code. Payment will not be deemed to have been made in full until we have collected good funds.

9.   Lots marked with □ immediately preceding the lot number are offered subject to a reserve, which is the confidential minimum price acceptable to the Consignor. No reserve will exceed the low presale estimate stated in the catalogue, or as amended by oral or posted notices. We may implement such reserve by opening the bidding on behalf of the Consignor and may bid up to the amount of the reserve, by placing successive or consecutive bids for a lot, or bids in response to other bidders. In instances where we have an interest in the lot other than our commission, we may bid up to the reserve to protect such interest. In certain instances, the Consignor may pay us less than the standard commission rate where a lot is "bought-in" to protect its reserve.

10.   Unless exempted by law, the purchaser will be required to pay the combined New York State and local sales tax, any applicable compensating use tax of another state, and if applicable, any federal luxury or other tax, on the total purchase price. The rate of such combined tax is 8¼% in New York City and ranges from 4% to 8½% elsewhere in New York.

11.   These Conditions of Sale and Terms of Guarantee, as well as the purchaser's and our respective rights and obligations hereunder, shall be governed by and construed and enforced in accordance with the laws of the State of New York. By bidding at an auction, whether present in person or by agent, order bid, telephone or other means, the purchaser shall be deemed to have consented to the exclusive jurisdiction of the state courts of, and the federal courts sitting in, the State of New York.

12.   We are not responsible for the acts or omissions in our packing or shipping of purchased lots or of other carriers or packers of purchased lots, whether or not recommended by us. Packing and handling of purchased lots is at the entire risk of the purchaser. If we obtain on behalf of the purchaser an export

license for an item containing an endangered species, there will be a charge of $150 for each license obtained.

13.   In no event will our liability to a purchaser exceed the purchase price actually paid.

NOTICE

No reference to imperfections is made in individual catalogue descriptions of property offered for sale. All lots are sold "AS IS" in accordance with Paragraph 1 of the Conditions of Sale, and we make no representation or warranty as to the condition of any lot sold. We disclaim responsibility for, and prospective bidders should not rely on, any description in the catalogue or any other source, including without limitation any gemological report, of the condition, size or quality of any lot.

Anyone wishing further information on any of the property included in this catalogue may write or call the Jewelry Department (212) 606-7392.

During the auction, a color slide of each lot will be shown as it is sold. This is only to assist the audience and the slide is not meant to represent the actual size, color or quality of the item offered.

TERMS OF GUARANTEE

Sotheby's warrants the authenticity of Authorship of each lot contained in this catalogue on the terms and conditions set forth below.

1.   Definition of Authorship. "Authorship" is defined as the creator, period, culture, source of origin, as the case may be, as set forth in the **BOLD TYPE HEADING** of a lot in this catalogue, as amended by any oral or written salesroom notices or announcements. If there is a "Glossary" of terms in this catalogue, please note that any such heading represents a qualified statement or opinion and is not subject to these Terms of Guarantee. Sotheby's makes no warranties whatsoever, whether express or implied, with respect to any material in the catalogue, other than

that appearing in **BOLD TYPE HEADING** and subject to the exclusions in 5 and 6 below.

2. Guarantee Coverage. Subject to the exclusions in 5 and 6 below, Sotheby's warrants the Authorship (as defined above) of a lot for a period of five years from the date of sale of such lot and only to the original purchaser of record at the auction. If it is determined to Sotheby's satisfaction that the **BOLD TYPE HEADING** is incorrect, the sale will be rescinded as set forth in 3 and 4 below, provided the lot is returned to Sotheby's at the original selling location in the same condition in which it was at the time of sale. It is Sotheby's general policy, and Sotheby's shall have the right to have the purchaser obtain, at the purchaser's expense, the opinion of two recognized experts in the field, mutually acceptable to Sotheby's and the purchaser, before Sotheby's determines whether to rescind a sale under the above warranty. If the purchaser requests, Sotheby's will provide the purchaser with the names of experts acceptable to it.

3. Non-Assignability. The benefits of this warranty are not assignable and shall be applicable only to the original purchaser of record and not to any subsequent owners (including, without limitation, heirs, successors, beneficiaries or assigns) who have, or may, acquire an interest in any purchased property.

4. Sole Remedy. It is specifically understood and agreed that the rescission of a sale and the refund of the original purchase price paid (the successful bid price, plus the buyer's premium) is exclusive and in lieu of any other remedy which might otherwise be available as a matter of law, or in equity. Sotheby's and the consignor shall not be liable for any incidental or consequential damages incurred or claimed.

5. Exclusions. This warranty does not apply to: (i) Authorship of any paintings, drawings or sculpture created prior to 1870, unless the lot is determined to be a counterfeit (a modern forgery intended to deceive) which has a value at the date of the claim for rescission which is materially less than the purchase price paid for the lot; or (ii) any catalogue description where it was specifically mentioned that there is a conflict of specialist opinion on the Authorship of a lot; or (iii) Authorship which on the date of sale was in accordance with the then generally accepted opinion of scholars and specialists; or (iv) the identification of

periods or dates of execution which may be proven inaccurate by means of scientific processes not generally accepted for use until after publication of the catalogue, or which were unreasonably expensive or impractical to use.

6. Limited Warranty. As stated in paragraph 1 of the Conditions of Sale, neither Sotheby's nor the Consignor makes any express or implied representations or warranties whatsoever concerning any property in the catalogue, including without limitation, any warranty of merchantability or fitness for a particular purpose, except as specifically provided herein.

Selling commissions are set and depend upon the value of a total consignment, together with the value of any previous consignment in a prior year. Thus, the seller at auction can take advantage of the art-world equivalent of "frequent-flier miles," an indication of the auction houses' desire to acquire brand loyalty from their regular consignors. Selling rates in September 1995 were as appears in the sample document (page 138).

As has been previously mentioned, the amount that the seller contributes to the sales costs will depend on the extent of the value and the attractiveness of the property, but these costs will be regularly borne by the consignor in consignments of under $1 million. It stands to reason that the higher the value, the more negotiable these costs become, recognizing that one hundred items worth $10,000 each are much more costly to sell than one item worth $1 million.

Timing

The question of when to sell has major implications for the seller. First, it must be understood that the art market as a whole is subject to fluctuation like any other market.

Although this broad movement of the art market is related to the movement of other markets such as the stock market, it is also subject to its own vagaries as well. This is in part due to the international nature of many of the segments of the art market and should come as no surprise that each element of the art market tends to follow its individualized path. The market in major French impressionists will be affected by the presence or absence of Japanese buyers, whereas the market in American furniture is unaffected by the ups and downs of the Tokyo stock exchange. On top of this, there are those who believe that the art market in certain areas is almost countercyclical in that weakness in monetary investments may lead people to invest in more tangible assets such as gold and antiques. Financial pressure can lead to selling, and major collections do come onto the market when an individual collector has suffered a serious economic reversal. However, any sense of distress selling may lead to bargain hunting on the part of buyers, and it does not help a property to appear under an economic cloud. I think it is more evident that good times in the money markets lead to increased enthusiasm in auction buying as collectors take advantage of increased discretionary funds. If the seller is not under immediate pressure to sell, then it is well worth taking a careful reading of the state of the art market overall. A direct question to a responsible member of the auction house should elicit some guidance in this area.

Institutional sellers and estates may have less discretion over the timing of sales since they may be under a deadline to realize the value of their assets. Under normal circumstances, the art market is not sufficiently volatile for timing to be of acute importance, especially if the property is of high quality and is coming fresh to the market. The art market is usually hungry for good examples and important masters. Immediate sale at least eliminates the ever-present possibility of a downturn in the market,

SELLING RATES, SEPTEMBER 5, 1995

New Vendor's Commission Rates

UNITED STATES

For sales beginning September 5, 1995, the commission rate charged on sales of $100,000 or more will be based upon the total amount of property a consignor sold at Sotheby's in the prior calendar year, or the rate applicable to the current consignment, whichever is lower. These commissions will be charged on a consignment, rather than a per lot basis. On consignments of less than $100,000, commission rates remain unchanged and will continue to be charged on a per lot basis.

DOLLAR AMOUNT	PRIVATE	NEW RATES		
		DEALER	MUSEUM	
$0–$99,999	20% to $1,999 15% from $2000–$7,499 10% above $7,500	15% to $1,999 10% from $2000–$7,499 6% above $7,500	15% to $1,999 10% from $2000–$7,499 6% above $7,500	
$100,000–$249,999	9.0%	6.0%	5.0%	
$250,000–$499,999	8.0%	6.0%	5.0%	
$500,000–$999,999	6.0%	6.0%	5.0%	

$1,000,000–$2,499,999	5.0%	5.0%	3.0%
$2,500,000–$4,999,999	4.0%	4.0%	2.0%
$5,000,000–$9,999,999	2.0%	2.0%	2.0%
$10,000,000–$24,999,999	lower of 2% OR 50% of expenses	lower of 2% OR 50% of expenses	lower of 2% OR 50% of expenses
$25,000,000 +	lower of (2% up to $25 million and 1% on any amount over $25 million) OR 50% of expenses	lower of (2% up tp $25 million and 1% on any amount over $25 million) OR 50% of expenses	lower of (2% up to $25 million and 1% on any amount over $25 million) OR 50% of expenses

Consignment related expenses, such as those for insurance and illustrations, will continue to be charged to sellers at the current rates.

while at the same time preventing any sharing in a potential upswing.

When it comes to the question of what time to sell within a particular season, each area is subject to traditional times for important sales. In New York, for example, the major impressionist sales are in the beginning of November and in the middle of May; the most important old-master paintings are sold in January; the important-American-paintings sales occur in October and late May; and so forth. Buying clients become accustomed to these traditional dates and make their travel plans around them. If the seller has a major item, it is worth waiting for the appropriate sale.

As has been discussed, a further issue surrounds major collections that are already scheduled for sale at a particular time. Here it is not always easy to determine whether a property will gain from association with some masterpieces, suffer from the comparison, or create too big a supply against a measurably limited demand. Since the auction house makes the greatest profit from the highest prices, it can be relied upon to offer sound advice when it comes to timing. The seller should, however, beware of an auction house that has failed to win a big property using another property under consideration to respond to the opposition's star sale. It knows that the star sale will outshine the property under consideration, but the auction house does not wish to appear empty the week of the other house's big sale. The argument that the house with the lesser property will give the seller's work closer attention does not in my opinion mitigate the potential damage of offering up a perfectly good but unspectacular property head to head with an outright star, even when the two properties are appearing in separate auction rooms. Two star properties will not detract from one another, providing the quality is equal.

Estimates and Reserves

The "Guide for Prospective Buyers," previously quoted, not only offers a good description of an estimate, but provides a useful introduction to the subject: "Each lot in the catalogue is given a low and high estimate. The estimates are guides for prospective bidders and, where possible, reflect prices that similar objects have sold for in the past. The estimates are determined several months before a sale and are therefore subject to revision to reflect current market conditions. Estimates should not be relied upon as a representation or prediction of actual selling prices. If you have any questions concerning a lot, please contact the specialist in charge of the sale whose name is printed in the front of this catalogue."

The seller needs to remember this role of the estimate—as a guide to the buyer, putting the buyer in the range within which other similar items have sold rather then determining the actual price of a lot. The seller should also note that high estimates do not make high prices. Rather the reverse. Prospective buyers are concerned that high estimates reflect high reserves, imposed under pressure by demanding consignors, and tend to shy away from bidding. Experience shows that reasonable estimates make high prices since buyers, who know that the reserve cannot exceed the low estimate, will be encouraged to bid where the estimates seem reasonable. The seller is reminded that there is nothing to prevent prospective buyers from bidding above the high estimate. The important thing is to get them involved in the bidding in the first place.

Most items in the salesroom are protected by a reserve, also known as a minimum or an upset price. As the catalogue states: "A reserve is the confidential minimum price established between Sotheby's and the seller. The reserve is generally set at a percentage of the low estimate and will not exceed the low estimate of the lot."

The seller is advised to set as reasonable a reserve as possible. The idea of a reserve is to protect an item in the event that there is no interest in that lot. It does not work as an artificial booster of the price since buyers are sophisticated enough to know when they are being pushed by the auctioneer. Early on in the proceedings, having heard an expert's true opinion as to the value of a lot, the seller should decide whether or not he or she is willing to sell with a reserve set below that level or not and should proceed accordingly. Experience over the years has shown that the most intelligent reserve is 80 percent of the low estimate. In the course of normal business the auction rooms buy back between 15 percent and 20 percent of items offered. While "bought-in" items—that is, those items that fail to reach their reserves—can often be sold privately following a sale, the reputation of the piece is not enhanced by being bought back. Sellers are strongly advised, having once made the decision to sell based on informed and reasonable estimates, to allow the market to determine the actual selling price, accepting that while some items will exceed their estimates, others may not quite reach the low estimate. At the end of the day, the aggregate of the individual sales will reflect remarkable accuracy overall. What has been lost on the swings will usually be gained on the roundabouts. A reasonable consignor tends to wind up with the greater majority of his or her property successfully sold.

Payment

The first thing that a prospective buyer should bear in mind is that a "buyer's premium" is charged on the final price bid under the hammer. Currently, the premium is 15 percent of the successful bid price up to and including

$50,000 and 10 percent on any amount in excess of $50,000.

In addition, purchasers should remember that, unless exempted by law, they will be required to pay the combined New York State and local taxes, any applicable compensating use tax of another state, and, if applicable, any federal luxury or other tax on the total purchase price. When purchasers reside out of state, they may avoid the New York State tax, but they become liable for their local taxes, which in most cases are significantly lower than those of New York State and New York City. Sotheby's collects taxes on purchases shipped to California, Connecticut, Florida, Illinois, Massachusetts, Minnesota, New Jersey, Pennsylvania, and Washington, D.C.

The auction houses expect immediate payment and will not deliver purchases until payment is received, unless credit arrangements have been provided in advance. The auction rooms have joined the age of plastic, and payment may be made by cash, check, or credit card up to certain limits, the latter being presented in person to be acceptable.

Regular clients are in the habit of establishing credit with the auction houses, arranging for check acceptance in advance and creating a credit record with the house. In certain cases, extended credit can be arranged. These arrangements must be made prior to the auction since the consignor must be contacted to establish whether he or she is willing to extend credit or not. Most consignors are reasonable in this regard since the establishment of extended credit very likely creates a new bidder on the lot involved. A typical arrangement would be for the successful purchaser to make three equal payments 30, 60, and 90 days following the sale.

In order to participate in a sale, a bidder must register and receive a numbered paddle. This registration is for identification purposes and can be accomplished with two forms of identification. It is not a credit check as such. Therefore, if a prospective bidder is intending to make a major purchase, he or she would be well advised to make credit arrangements with the auction house prior to the sale.

Each sales catalogue contains the names of the auction-house representatives responsible for buying, shipping, and selling. These agents are in place to help the prospective buyer with every aspect of the process. Their help is available at no charge, and the seasoned auctiongoer makes full use of their services.

The consignor will normally receive the proceeds of sale, less commissions and any other charges, 35 days following the sale. Obviously, if extended payment has been arranged, as outlined above, the auction house will pay under the terms agreed upon. While payment will normally be made in the currency of the country in which the sale has taken place, arrangements can be made to pay in the currency of the consignor's choice and to any bank he or she wishes. Unusual payment procedures should be put in place as early as possible. Most auctioneers will be unwilling to make settlements in cash but are willing to pay third-party nominees upon valid written instruction.

Payments to the consignor usually require the purchaser to have paid the auction house. However, if the auction house has already released the property to the purchaser, the auction house becomes liable for the settlement to the consignor, whether the auction house has received payment or not. The auction house will make sustained efforts to collect from purchasers, often beyond the limits of its legal obligation, but it also retains the right to cancel a sale, retaining the property for either return to the owner or to be reoffered at a later date, should payment fail to be forthcoming. The auction house will contact the consignor in such cases to determine which course the consignor wishes to pursue.

All this sounds somewhat alarming, but the consignor and buyer should both recognize that the vast majority of transactions take place without any complications. The auction houses have huge staffs to ensure that business is conducted with due efficiency and dispatch. The incredible amount of transactions successfully completed each year is attributable to highly sophisticated accounting methods and advanced use of computer capabilities. It is in fact possible to walk 50 yards from the salesroom, then pay for and pick up your purchase within five minutes of executing a successful bid.

III

How to Buy at Auction

Types of Buyers

While there are almost as many types of buyers as there are lots for sale, they may be categorized broadly into three distinctive segments: the private buyer, museums or institutions, and commercial dealers. Each of these constituencies will buy for its own purposes and reasons, which bear with a brief analysis.

The Private Buyer

Depending on their economic comfort range, private buyers may be anyone from a young married couple decorating their first apartment to a dedicated and highly knowledgeable collector in a particular esoteric field. While they practice at differing ends of the auction spectrum, they both have discovered the satisfaction of buying from a wide range of potential offerings and at a fair market price items that meet their needs. With a few notable exceptions, private collectors are indulging an avocation rather than a professional full-time commitment. For them, collecting is a hobby, albeit a hobby based on a continuing passion. It requires the expense of much time in study and research. The collector gains satisfaction from the thrill of the chase. With the passage of time, a notable collector who specializes in one area will gain an expertise similar to the dealer's and the cataloguer's through a continuous connection to an active market. The buying and selling of objects in an active market not only heighten the collector's awareness of market trends and values, but also allow the collector to upgrade the quality of a collection as expertise and knowledge deepen.

The broad variety of knowledge sought by the private collector has led auction houses to make extensive efforts to educate their buyers in every field of collecting. Newsletters, preview magazines, lectures, symposia, seminars, and published works all serve to help the private buyer enhance existing expertise. Salesrooms offer a wide variety of client services or customer advisory services in order to make the knowledge of the auction house more available. The buyer may consult any of these "account executives" free of charge, and, should they not know the answer to a question, they will certainly know to whom the question should be addressed, acting as a conduit to the cataloguers, departmental specialists, and a number of relevant sources of information such as restoration consultants. These agents will also assist in executing bids, answering questions as to condition, and consulting on any changes in the presale estimates. They can also help make shipping and other arrangements in the event of a successful purchase. The private buyer, especially if new to the auction method, is strongly advised to seek out one of these customer-service agents should the buyer wish to bid regularly. A buyer may, for instance, give such an agent a "wish list" of items he or she is hoping to acquire. The agent keeps an eye on the salesroom and lets the potential buyer know when a possible item appears. With the great proliferation in the number of sales, this service can be invaluable to the private collector, who typically has a job to do during the day.

Taken as a broad group and recognizing that each area produces widely differing statistics, private buyers account for well over 50 percent of auction purchases. Many who attend auctions may not be coming initially as buyers, but rather as spectators, using the auction room as a place to learn how to distinguish quality and value as well as an accurate indicator of the current state of a given market. All are welcome to attend an auction, and, with the exception of the highly important impressionist and modern sales, no tickets are required. There is no question that auctions make a fascinating spectator sport. The auction houses acknowledge this, encouraging attendance in the firm belief that such initial voyeurism will eventually lead to active participation.

The presale exhibition provides an ideal learning tool for the private collector. Here, identification and discernment skills are sharpened without the need to spend money. The auction houses recognize that the interested neophyte of today is the hardened collector of tomorrow. Collecting could be described as a chronic, contagious, terminal disease for which no known cure has yet been established. Auction rooms harbor vast quantities of this contagion.

Museums and Institutional Collectors

The institutional buyer, be it a museum, library, college, or other cultural establishment, serves several functions in the auction market. The institution supplies scholarly and academic expertise in its field of endeavor. Scholars frequently spend a lifetime concentrating on the work of one artist or a small group of artists, sometimes being responsible for the creation of catalogues raisonnes, complete listings of a given artist's works. Such information is an invaluable asset to the auction-house specialist and cataloguer.

The institution also helps to identify quality in an area of collecting. When properly managed, a museum will seek to acquire only the rarest and best examples available in a field. In this way, the institution sets an example in quality. From the point of view of the market, this creates an interesting corollary effect. By acquiring the very best examples as they appear on the open market, the museum withdraws them from circulation in the market, thereby reducing the supply of similar items and thus increasing the demand and raising the value of those works that remain on the open market.

Where a particular field contains a solidly finite supply, the effect is apparent, as is evident in the example of American eighteenth-century furniture. Produced in its most desirable form in the period between 1760 and 1790, this beautiful furniture was manufactured in less than ten centers on the eastern seaboard for a remarkably few wealthy householders. Bearing in mind a total population of some 2 million throughout the country at that time, of whom the vast majority could not afford fine furniture—they were too busy struggling to survive—some idea of the small size of the supply emerges. Today, in a population of over 250 million, more and more collectors are appearing with the ability to spend significant sums in this popular field. Most major American cities, especially those in which the eighteenth-century furniture was originally manufactured, support museums that actively attempt to acquire fine representative collections of American furniture. This competitive desire, often encouraged and supported by wealthy local private collectors, has led to a steady and spectacular increase in the value of such American furniture, with prices in excess of $1 million ceasing to be a surprise. The role of the great museums in the art market is major and vital to the health of the market.

Dealers: The Professional Art Merchants

The extraordinary knowledge and experience of reputable dealers place them in a strategic position as buyers in the auction rooms. Dealers survive economically on the basis of the accuracy of their judgments. The auction rooms are for them a supply of marketable property that must be bought sufficiently reasonably to pass on to a client at a respectable profit. Clients will be willing to pay the premium involved because they are paying for the dealer's knowledge, experience, and warranty of authenticity, allowing clients a degree of assurance that they might not feel should they go it alone. In a reputable dealer, this premium is often well spent, especially in the case of the inexperienced collector.

The dealer buying at auction may be doing so for a number of purposes. The purchase may be for stock, where an item fits in with the gallery's type of inventory and has been made as a form of speculation, in which the dealer hopes to turn the item around for a profit in a reasonable amount of time but has no immediate client in mind. The dealer may also be bidding at an auction sale as a direct agent for a collector, either as a courtesy or for a predetermined fee. In the case of bidding on behalf of a client, there are various factors to be considered. The collector's anonymity is preserved, preventing the competition from pushing a known collector to pay a higher price in order to discourage them from bidding for themselves at auction. The dealer will also offer the client advice as to quality, condition, bidding levels, and other factors regarding the potential purchase. The commissions paid for these services vary but usually fall between 2 percent and 5 percent, depending on how extensive the assistance might be and on the price level of the item involved. It is not unknown for the dealer to execute a bid on an important item free of charge. The successful dealer in these circumstances may expect considerable free publicity and exposure, which can only accrue to the dealer's benefit.

There is another major advantage for commissioning a dealer to bid on behalf of a private collector. In executing a bid for a client, the dealer is in effect eliminated from the competition with that client on a lot in which both parties may have had an interest. An intelligent collector would rather pay a small commission to a bidding agent than run the risk of battling with a professional in the auction arena. Active collectors can definitely avoid paying higher prices by preserving their anonymity. The dealer's knowledge of appropriate bidding levels is likely to be extremely accurate, although no one can foresee the new bidding levels that can be achieved by an item of supreme quality coming fresh onto the market. The dealers do not get carried away by the occasion. They arrive at a sale knowing what their bidding limits are, unwilling to be pressured by the heat of the moment. This is sound business practice that private buyers would be wise to imitate.

It is fascinating to watch a professional dealer view a sale at auction. The inspection is thorough and the concentration remarkable. Every facet of an item is noted and a decision reached on the highest practicable bid. Thus, the decision has been made before the actual auction begins. A dealer will, nevertheless, be prepared to adjust his or her bid according to the observed activity of the market on the day of sale. A movement in the salesroom market may lead to an adjustment of price levels in the gallery, both upward or downward. The presence of these professionals is a vital element in the successful auction sale, guaranteeing a minimum price level and ensuring regular activity in each field. It can be truly said that the relationship of the dealer to the auction house is one of interdependence. The dealers need the auction room to establish new price levels and to maintain a constant supply of materials, and the auction house needs the dealers to provide a solid base of professional buyers.

Reading the Catalogue

Much energy is put into the creation of the auction catalogue. It is, after all, the major marketing tool for the auction house. It is also the principal source of information for the buyer. Although some of what is about to be said is repetitive, I believe that it is worthwhile to conduct a systematic tour of a catalogue in order to point out to the reader some of the uses to which this multifaceted document can be put. For this purpose, I have chosen *Magnificent Jewelry from a Private Collection* because it is the most recent catalogue produced at the time of writing. The interior style will be out of date by the time this book is published, but the basic contents, while rearranged, will remain similar.

The cover itself bears some attention. It will always contain a definition of the type of sale—in this case, jewelry—and the date of the sale, an important feature that can be checked without having to pore through the catalogue. In the case of important sales, the cover will give the name of the consignor, if it is a "single owner" catalogue. In a general catalogue, the owners' names, where they may be used, are placed in the context of their particular lots. Since, as we have already established, provenance is important, careful note should be made of these names. In most categories, the use of the adjectives *Important, Fine, Magnificent, Highly Important* will serve to advise the potential buyer of how the property rates on the informal "Richter scale" of importance bestowed upon the property by the auction house. Cynics might suggest that this scale of hyperbole is merely an indicator of how expensive the items are. Given the need to retain credibility and in spite of the admitted marketing component of this use, I would still maintain that the highest quality is likely to be found in those catalogues that have received the most superlative accolade.

On opening the catalogue and reaching the title page, the reader is faced with much more detailed and useful information (see page 153 for Sample Catalogue Title Page). The sales number, which also appears on the spine of the cover, is listed. This number is important in all com-

Magnificent Jewelry from a Private Collection

Sale 6757

AUCTION

Wednesday, October 25, 1995 at 2pm

EXHIBITION

Friday, October 20	1 pm to 4:45 pm
Saturday, October 21	10 am to 4:45 pm
Sunday, October 22	1 pm to 5 pm
Monday, October 23	10 am to 4:45 pm
Tuesday, October 24	10 am to 4:45 pm
Wednesday, October 25	10 am to 12 noon

For your convenience we will be accepting
appointments for dealer viewing.
Please contact Frank E. Cruet (212) 606-7392

ABSENTEE BIDS

This catalogue may be referred to as 6757 "PRINCE"
Fax (for bids only): (212) 606-7016

Front Cover Illustration: Lot 79
Back Cover Illustration: Lot 1

Catalogue $25 at the gallery, $32 by mail, $39 overseas

munications with the auction house, verifying, for instance, that your bid is being placed on the right sale. The day, date, and time of the auction appear next. In this instance, the auction is being conducted in one session, but in many cases, a sale may have multiple sessions. Impressionist sales, for instance, start with an evening session, often at 7:30 P.M., continue the next morning at 10:15 A.M., and finish with a third session at 2:00 P.M. the same day. It goes without saying that there is nothing more frustrating for a bidder than to arrive either on the wrong day or at the wrong time for a sale, thereby missing an opportunity to bid. Auction houses used to add the word "precisely" after the set times. While this word has disappeared from usage, it is a general policy to begin on time since the number of lots placed in a session require sales to start on time in order to end before the close of business. This is not a major deal with a sale such as the one under discussion, with only 107 lots, but auctioneers in the lower-level sales are used to selling up to 300 lots in a session, which works out to nearly 2 per minute. To achieve this, the sale has to start on time.

The next information to appear is the exhibition schedule. Generally speaking, a property will be on view for five days. Depending on how much other property is on view, this exhibition may occasionally last as long as a week. Since viewing is a vital part of preparing to bid at auction, the potential buyer should note with care the times of the exhibition. In the case of this jewelry sale, as with many other categories, it is stated that dealers may make appointments for viewing independently of this schedule. Not only dealers, but established private buyers may always apply to view property, both during and before the public exhibition, by applying directly to the department involved. It does not take a department very long to establish if such inquiries are serious, and successful subsequent purchases are the best proof of intention.

Every sale has not only a number, but also a code

name—in this case, "PRINCE." This code name is a double check for accuracy in the case of submitted bids. The client states both the code name and the number so that there is absolute certainty as to which sale is referred to. If these two do not jibe, the auction house will get back to the client.

The front and back cover lots are referred to as an obvious way to tie a potential buyer to a lot that has attracted him or her from the illustrations on the cover. Referral to the actual catalogue description is essential in order for the buyer to be made aware of the important information contained in the catalogue description.

The price of the catalogue is then given. These prices seem exorbitant, but, when the amount of color work is considered, they compare appropriately with art books of similar quality. However, the auction houses would much prefer that a client subscribe to one or more categories of catalogue on an annual basis. This can be done relatively inexpensively and ties the client in to a whole series of mailings that will keep her or him informed of the auction house's activities, both in the specialized field involved and in other areas.

There follows the name of the auction house, which might prevent a client from going to the competition by mistake (it occasionally happens), together with the address, which is useful for the first-timer, and a general telephone number. Much more useful telephone numbers appear later in the text, but this general number is effective during normal office hours. The final statement on the page is the name and license number of the principal auctioneer. This is a legal requirement and does not indicate that Mr. Ruprecht, in this instance, will be taking this jewelry sale. It would be cumbersome to list all the auctioneers since there are some 20 of us. In fact, it is highly likely that John Block, who is the director of the Jewelry Department, will be taking this sale. Should he be prevented by sickness or otherwise from doing so, there are several other auctioneers well able to wield the gavel on this occasion, and the auction house maintains backup availability in case of emergency. Who takes which sale will be the topic of discussion when the role of the auctioneer is discussed.

The next two pages are nothing more than a detailed telephone directory, by which the client is enabled to be in touch with everyone at the auction house involved in the particular sale without having to go through an arduous telephone search. International clients are, thus, able to contact their local branch offices in order to acquire information or to arrange for the transaction of absentee bids. Condition reports and detailed estimates may also be channeled through these local offices. With major sales, there may also be a traveling exhibition. The branch offices will know this schedule and can help clients with details of these opportunities to view highlights from a sale without having to travel to a major auction center. Educational studies in the particular area are also listed, affording the private client an opportunity to expand his or her knowledge in the field. The second page of telephone numbers lists the names of all the auction-house employees specifically designated to assist clients in the sale: Client Advisory Services, Absentee Bids, Client Services Desk (which is actually on the exhibition floor), 24 Hour Recorded Information (essential in an international business, given the changes of time zones), Payment and Shipping, and, finally, Catalogue Subscriptions. While there is no substitute for attending the exhibition and sale oneself, with these numbers it is perfectly possible to participate in a sale from the other side of the world, having viewed the property with the aid of a professional-quality color transparency.

The next two pages take the form of a more general telephone directory, listing all the expert departments, giving a full outline of the Client Services operation, and listing the various administrative departments. Using this directory, the client is able to find out who is responsible for a particular part of a transaction. Since the auction business is essentially a service business, the people listed know that they are subject to calls by clients at any time. While some of the titles may appear mysterious to the newcomer, most of them are self-explanatory. Any misdirected calls will usually be transferred with a minimum of fuss to the appropriate destination.

The four pages that describe the "Conditions of Sale," the "Terms of Guarantee," the "Guide for Prospective Buyers," and the "Guide for Prospective Sellers," have already been covered (see pages 130, 134, 114, and 110, respectively). Further information on "Appraisals," "Financial Services," and "Catalogues, Price Lists and Newsletter" is added at this point, all of which will be covered in a later section of this book.

These pages are followed by a page containing the "masthead" of the company, the officers of the auction house responsible for the conduct of business. Here is a mixture of business management skill, senior expertise, and international connections. All these constituencies perform a function in making the international auction business a success. Serious collectors would want to consider getting to know the relevant people from this group. Over the years, friendships develop, and collecting leads to a more personal involvement with those who have made a lifetime commitment to participating in the fascinating world of fine-arts auctions. After thirty-five years in the business, I could not imagine a more interesting group of business associates than those listed on this page. A fascinating book could be written using only the characters who appear here. It would be a book that has to await retirement, but the temptation remains strong.

"Important Notices," which follow, should always be read with care. They reflect particular conditions pertaining to the sale under consideration. Such matters as the frame of reference on condition and disclaimers over stone processes are addressed, when they are not covered by the standard conditions of sale. Buyers must be sure to understand the precise conditions under which they are bidding in order to avoid later confusion, not to mention legal animosity.

The final page prior to the catalogue itself takes the form of an introduction, often to be found in the case of major one-owner sales. This introduction is written either by a close friend or associate of the consignor or by one of the experts from the auction house with a close tie to the collection. In the case of the catalogue under review, the introduction was written by His Royal Highness Prince Dimitri of Yugoslavia, who not only was instrumental in bringing the sale to auction, but is also employed as a jewelry specialist by Sotheby's. Fifteen pages into the catalogue, the reader finally reaches the catalogue descriptions themselves.

The sales catalogue itself provides precise descriptions of each lot in the order in which the sale will take place, together with facts such as measurements and weights, where appropriate. The purpose of the description, often in conjunction with the illustration, is to identify an item in such a way that it cannot possibly be confused with any other similar item. Each expert department invokes its own specialized language, which follows traditional formulas when it comes to describing a work. Signatures and other distinguishing marks are noted. Many catalogues also have background notes to particular lots. These notes contain useful information, reflecting the depth of expertise of the experts and greatly adding to the knowledge of the potential buyer. Earlier, I gave as an example of one of the fullest forms of catalogue entries that for the Medici birth salver (see pages 97–108). Most descriptions do not need this amount of detail, and buyers become suspicious when the elaborate nature of the description exceeds the apparent quality of a lot. Most buyers are from the "just give us the facts" school and resent a catalogue that

spends too much time describing in highfalutin jargon
what is perfectly evident from the catalogue illustration.
Buyers should beware of the extreme difficulty in repro-
ducing color accurately. In spite of every effort made to
produce faithful illustrations, it has to be emphasized that
color illustrations provide just an approximation of the
actual color of a work under certain specific lighting conditions. Visual inspection remains the only sure method
of assessing color, although color transparencies are considerably more accurate than the printed illustrations in
the catalogue.

Each catalogue description is followed by the presale
estimate, which has already been discussed. The buyer is
reminded that the presale estimate is initially given several months prior to the sale, usually when the item is first
inspected. This original estimate is often adjusted following detailed examination and cataloguing, but this last
adjustment will still be made at least two months before
the actual sales date. Printers' deadlines and the need for
the catalogues to receive at least a month's circulation
guarantee some removal from the time of the estimate to
the actual conditions prevalent on the date of sale. Thus,
it is always appropriate to ask the auction rooms if there
have been any updates on the estimate or whether market
conditions have changed significantly since the catalogue
was "put to bed." This explains why a few major lots are
accompanied by the statement "Estimate upon request"
or "Refer department." In these cases, the department will
adjust the estimate in reflection of the precise conditions
and the interest displayed in order to give the potential
buyer the most accurate information available. Buyers in
this range of value would be well advised to make the call
and, should they wish to retain anonymity, make the call
through an agent.

As a convenience to buyers who collect works by certain artists, craftsmen, or manufacturers, many catalogues
offer an index following the catalogue section. These in-

dexes are also useful for those who wish to review the results of a sale in certain areas since the published price list and the index combined can rapidly put the collector in touch with current price trends. There are also several computerized auction price services now available in which the searching is done for the subscriber automatically. The challenge with these computer listings is that they do not provide the full descriptions and illustrations that form an essential element in assessing the current value of particular works of art.

In the jewelry catalogue under review, there follows a "Guide for Absentee Bidders," which enumerates the auction house's policies with regard to this important function. With advances in technology, more and more bidders are executing their bids without coming to the sale itself. This has become a sophisticated and safe way to execute bids, which can be handled in a number of ways. A client may fill out an "Absentee Bid Form," which can be removed from the back of the catalogue or which may be obtained at the auction house (see pages 162–163). This form lists the essential information concerning the client and his or her relationship to the auction house, as well as methods and conditions for payment. The form requires the signature of the client, authorizing the auction house to make a bid on the client's behalf. It is important to note that the auction house agrees to execute the bid *as cheaply as possible* against the bids in the room, thereby removing the fear that the auctioneer will run the bidding up to the absentee bidder's limit. This absentee bid may either be entered into the auctioneer's catalogue or may be executed in the room by a member of the Bids Department, who, once again, will represent the client and attempt to buy the item at the lowest possible price. A bidding representative will always be used if an absentee bidder registers what is called an "either / or" bid, in which the client will say, "I bid $2,000 on lot 1. If I fail to buy lot 1, then I bid $1,500 on lot 16," or any one of many variations on this theme, such as, "I bid as follows on the ten lots listed, but wish to stop when I have spent $10,000." It is illegal to process a "buy bid," in which the auction house is told by a client to buy an item "at any price," the implications of which hardly need explaining other than to suggest that there may be someone in the room with the same instructions. The results, while dramatic, are not, in the end, going to enhance an auction house's reputation for fair dealing.

An alternative method of absentee bidding, becoming more popular as telephone services improve, is that of bidding by telephone on an open line. Arrangements are made with the auction house ahead of time, and one of the client services representatives places the call a few lots ahead of the lot or lots in which the client is interested. In this way, the client can bid against the room at the actual sale, being made aware as the sale progresses as to how the bidding is going and retaining the ability to adjust his or her own bidding to the action in the room. Major sales now involve large numbers of telephone bidders, increasing the activity, while, it has to be admitted, slowing down the bidding while telephone bidders respond to the salesroom bids. A very significant percentage of property is now being bought over the phone, which, apart from providing the convenience of bidding from one's home, which might be anywhere in the world, also gives the telephone buyer the advantage of anonymity. The bidding booths that surround Sotheby's salesroom in New York, a feature unique to these rooms, also provide such anonymity as buyers watch the competition from their individual "fish tanks" and communicate their bids by interior telephone to one of the auction-house employees in the salesroom. These particular bidders are, thus, both absent and present at the same time.

Shipment arrangements are then specified for the convenience of buyers. Clearly, the international nature of the business leads to many complications in this area. The

ABSENTEE BID FORM

SALE TITLE   **Magnificent Jewelry from a Private Collection**

DATE   **October 25, 1995 at 2pm**

SALE CODE   **"PRINCE" 6757**

Name *(please print or type)*

Date

☐ Sotheby's Card #   ☐ Sotheby's Account #

Address

City   State   Zip Code   Telephone

                                                           Fax

☐ Please check if this is a new address.

PAYMENT NOTE: If you wish to pay for any purchase made by absentee bid with a credit or charge card, you must present the card in person to Sotheby's. To pay with the American Express ® Card, please complete an Advance Form (available at the Purchaser Accounting Desk) before the auction and, if your bid is successful, within five days after the auction sign and return (in person, by fax or courier) a confirming invoice (which Sotheby's will provide to you).

Bank reference or deposit *(if bidder is unknown to Sotheby's)*

I agree that I am bound by the "Conditions of Sale" and "Terms of Guarantee" if applicable, which are published in the catalogue for the sale and govern all purchases at auction that I make.

Signed
(We must have your signature to execute this bid.)

Lot Number   Item

....

....

....

....

....

....

....

....

Sotheby's
1334 York Avenue
New York, N.Y. 10021
Bid Department (212) 606-7414

IMPORTANT
Please see "Guide for Absentee Bidders" opposite this sheet.

I wish to place the following bids for this sale to
be held on October 25, 1995. These bids are to
be executed by Sotheby's up to but not exceeding the amount or amounts specified below.
Each bid is PER LOT, as indicated, and all bids
will be executed and are accepted subject to the
"Conditions of Sale" and "Terms of Guarantee"
printed in the catalogue of this sale. Please note
that a buyer's premium in the amount stated in
paragraph 3 of the "Conditions of Sale" in the
front of this catalogue will be added to the hammer price as part of the total purchase price.

ARRANGING PAYMENT
In order to avoid delays in receiving purchases,
buyers unknown to us are advised to make payment arrangements or supply credit references
in advance of the sale date. If such arrangements are not made, purchases cannot leave our
premises until checks have been cleared.

PLEASE MAIL OR FAX TO
Sotheby's Bid Department
1334 York Avenue
New York, N.Y. 10021

FAX (212) 606-7016

Top Limit of Bid not including the buyer's
premium (Bid is per lot number as listed in
the catalogue)

$

$

$

$

$

$

$

$

auction houses run departments that specialize in all aspects of the shipping, export, and delivery of works of art. It is essential to ask the auction house to provide an estimate of the shipping costs involved, which it is ready to do over the telephone. In some cases, the auction house will refer the buyer to specialized outside shipping agents, whose use is strongly urged. Amateur packing and shipping not only place works of art at unnecessary risk, but the savings in costs are minimal.

Every sales catalogue contains the "Absentee Bid Form," already discussed. The advantage of using the form in the catalogue is that it is "sales-specific," containing the sales number and code name of the sale itself, thereby further eliminating the risk that the bid could be placed in the wrong sale.

The final pages of the catalogue contain a listing of the "International Auction Locations and Representatives" of the auction room and, in the case of American-based catalogues, a listing of all the North American offices. This gentle form of advertisement not only gives the client some sense of the worldwide scope of the auction house's reach, but, again, gives the client information as to the availability of the auction house's services at every major center throughout the world. The collector is never far away from an auction-house representative, whose services go far beyond the buying and selling of works of art at auction, as will be discussed later.

It can, therefore, be seen that the auction catalogue forms an essential part of the collector's equipment, not only in providing the precise information necessary to make a decision as to whether or not to bid on a particular item, but as a permanent record of activity within a given market. As items in the art market eventually recirculate, the ability to trace them back through previous appearances at auction remains an important facet in establishing current value. There is no better way to learn the equation of quality to value than a trip through some major back catalogues, particularly the important single-owner sales. Since most collecting areas contain a relatively finite number of works of the highest quality, this task is fairly easily achieved and tremendously rewarding, part of the basic research of a well-informed collector. The new collector is advised to start with old catalogues. They are the sine qua non of the educational process.

Asking the Right Questions

The questions the potential buyer should be asking will in many ways echo the questions that have already been studied, as we looked at the specialist's mode of operation. However, when a potential purchase is being considered, these questions will assume a slightly different priority and will be joined with some additional questions arising from the particular nature of individual collections. Let us start with the questions surrounding the expertise of the collector.

Authenticity remains the foremost consideration. The manner in which the item is presented by the auction room will take the buyer most of the way, but I believe that the buyer should not suspend caution on the basis of the auction house's reputation and expertise. The knowledgeable buyer must develop that all-important sense that tells him or her when he or she is in the presence of the "real thing." Comparison with known similar works, either in museums or in other private collections, is one way of building up this vital skill of sensing authenticity. A discussion with the expert who wrote the catalogue entry is never wasted, including the question "What convinced you that this work is genuine?" a question that a reliable expert is only too happy to address.

The subject matter or form of the work of art should be given due consideration. If the objective of the collector is to assemble only pieces of the finest quality so that the collection can gain a reputation that will enhance its over-all value, then no compromises can be made. A work that is considered ugly or cumbersome, atypical or unlike any other work by the creator will never achieve the accep-tance of the attractive, immediately recognizable master-piece. Contrarians tend not to succeed in the art market. If a collector chooses to concentrate on unpopular subjects for whatever personal reason, he or she can expect to buy inexpensively but must also be prepared to sell inexpen-sively.

After authenticity, subject matter, and form, condition must be the single most important factor in determining whether or not a work belongs in a fine private collection. I believe that the collector can only expect trouble if any compromise is made in this matter. In most cases, the auction houses can render an accurate condition report, but, in the case of works of art of great importance or value, I would highly recommend the hiring of a highly qualified restorer in the appropriate field to render a pro-fessional written opinion as to quality. The time, money, and effort spent to acquire this opinion will be amply rewarded in the long run. The skilled private collector becomes used to rejecting that which was first enthusiasti-cally embraced when the technical report argues for hold-ing back. Success comes from learning to say no and waiting for the better example in prime condition to ap-pear on the market.

Most often, rarity will be a known factor to the educated collector. Beginners should carefully learn what consti-tutes rarity, a matter that varies considerably from cate-gory to category. Rarity is, at one time, the simple execution of the law of supply and demand and, in the art world, signifies a work that stands out in its own environ-ment and shows clear superiority to most other similar examples. The issues of provenance and historical sig-nificance may give an otherwise reasonably common work of art a rare quality. Lincoln's beaver hat is rare; my grandfather's lacks that quality.

Size has much to do with the nature of the individual collector's environment and collecting strategy. While extremes of size must be viewed with caution on account of the difficulties in resale, just as important is the consideration of the scale of the collection. If it is to be housed in a regular apartment, excessive size will not be appropriate. If, on the other hand, a collector has built a huge edifice to house what amounts to a private museum, then what better way to begin than with a huge masterpiece to set the style for the collection as the works are added? Had a private collector purchased Frederick Church's *Icebergs* (see Figure 34) and hung it as the first major acquisition in a new private museum, two immediate effects would have been noted. First, every serious student of American luminists would have had to make his or her way to the house in order to view this signal work, a great opportunity for the exchange of common interests. Second, the collector would immediately be noted as one with extremely serious interests in the field of nineteenth-century American painting and would be flooded with opportunities to buy other, similarly important works. Thus, I am suggesting that, once the initial homework and research have been accomplished, there is something to be said for "jumping into the deep end of the collecting pool," thereby making a splash that will be instantly noticed by the market. The auction house will be delighted to bring to the potential buyer's attention those works that have the capacity to achieve this effect.

The medium remains an important issue not only because different media attract differing levels of price, but because some artists' reputations are founded on their work in one medium over another. Winslow Homer was perhaps at his happiest in the watercolor medium, his prints attracting relatively little attention. Cassatt and Degas were great exponents of pastel, a medium that in most artists is less sought after. The difficulties of maintaining works in some media should be borne in mind. Works of art on paper cannot be hung in direct sunlight. And fine furniture of the eighteenth century cannot be safely maintained in sun-drenched climates. The climatic conditions in the country of origin should be remembered. Northern Europe in the seventeenth and eighteenth centuries, before the invention of central heating and air conditioning, presented the perfect conditions for the maintenance of this delicate woodwork, an average temperature of 50 degrees Fahrenheit, an average humidity of 50 percent, and less than 20 percent variation on these figures throughout the year. What, then, is to be expected from a New York apartment, with temperatures varying from 50 degrees to 100 degrees and humidity varying from 50 percent to 100 percent? Needless to add, Florida is even worse, particularly on the coastline, where the added menace of salt-sea spray adds a fatal nail to the condition coffin.

Having worked through these considerations, the collector is now faced with those questions created by the unique nature of the particular collection. Every collector needs to create a collecting strategy since it is impossible to collect everything, even in a specialized field. Thus, to return to the field of American furniture, is the collector going to concentrate on one center—Boston, Philadelphia, or Rhode Island, for example? Or does the collector restrict himself or herself to a particular form of furniture—case furniture, chairs, clocks, for instance? Let us say that the collector is attempting to reproduce an eighteenth-century American home in Philadelphia. Are one dining-room table and one card table sufficient? Can one add a portrait by Copley, even if it is less likely that he would have painted a commission in Philadelphia? To the extent that a collection can give a broad account of a particular area, it will gain a greater reputation if it is complete and well rounded. In a totally different field, that of Rembrandt etchings, an eventual and highly expensive strategy might be to acquire the best available states of every single etching that Rembrandt made, continually trading up as to quality as examples come onto the market. This exercise would require working capital of some $20 million, which, although a huge amount of money, remains reasonable compared with a similar strategy in French impressionist paintings. All of which is to say that I believe that a collector should not collect at random, but should, rather, develop a theme that gives the collection its character and unique quality. Not only will this give the collector greater satisfaction, but it will, in the long run, add measurably to the importance and value of the collection. Incidentally, once the direction of a collection becomes known, auction houses and dealers will keep their eyes open for items that will fit the collection and bring such opportunities to the attention of the collector. The art world is small enough for this practice to be extremely effective. This sharing of enthusiasm within a very specific area is one of the elements that makes collecting pleasurable, and it produces lasting friendships between like-minded collectors, dealers, and auction-house representatives.

Registration, Paddles, and Bidding

The view of the exhibition being completed, a few housekeeping details need to be taken care of before the day of the sale itself. If a potential buyer plans on making a substantial purchase, it is important to arrange credit in advance. This will ease the actual purchase procedure. The auction house is entitled to know the rough amount of credit the buyer seeks. Only if terms such as "30-60-90 days" are sought will it be necessary to divulge to the auction house which particular lots are of interest.

Sales are conducted with paddles, which are retained by the auction house until just prior to the sale. Regular customers arrive and just pick up their paddles on the way into the salesroom. New bidders will be required to provide two forms of identification. The paddle number is used to identify the eventual buyer of each lot. However, it is not necessary to make the bid with the paddle. Some customers prefer a more discreet approach to their bidding, and we will discuss the various forms these signals might take when we come to the auction itself. For now, it should be understood that you cannot bid unless you have registered, and when you register you have to accept a paddle with your temporary registration number on it. Since different colored paddles are used for each sale, this procedure must be repeated for each sale. Occasionally, two or more sales are taking place on the same day, often in different locations within the main building. Errant paddles have been known to appear after a successful bid. These are rapidly and easily replaced on the spot with the correct paddles by a client service representative. Failure to correct such an error could, of course, lead to a nightmare in the purchaser accounts area.

Duly registered, with credit established, and having already decided which lots are of interest, the customer checks the date, time, and location of the sale, arrives with enough time to spare to pick up a paddle, and walks into the salesroom, taking any seat that suits his or her fancy. It is time for the auction to begin. Six month's of preparation now narrow down to as little as half a minute. It is time to examine the anatomy of the auction itself.

IV

The Auction Adventure: What's Going On Here?

THE FIRST DECISION is where to sit. Those who want to see what is going on among the competing bidders usually sit toward the rear of the room. Those who wish to preserve anonymity and to have close rapport with the auctioneer or one of the bid spotters will sit near the front, which also offers the advantage of proximity to the items being sold. It must once more be emphasized that speculative bidding, based on the view from the auction room, without prior inspection, can only be regarded as foolhardy. In the final analysis, it is often hard to tell who is bidding no matter where one sits. It is a matter of personal taste, and, except in the most major of sales, there are no reserved sections or individual seats.

On entering the salesroom just prior to a sale, the newcomer will be amazed by how many people from the auction house are involved. Surely, all one needs is an auctioneer, a sale clerk to record the prices, and maybe two porters to carry the items on stage and off again. The sophistication of the big houses, however, involves a large number of people, not only those visible in the auction room, but many more behind the scenes, making sure that each item is in place, sold, and processed as rapidly as possible, ensuring a smooth flow of business and a minimum of customer aggravation. Let's take a look at this group of people in the auction room itself (see Figure 58).

The Cast of Characters

Registration Desk(s)

Either directly outside or immediately inside the salesroom will be found the registration desk, where potential

Figure 58. View of an auction room with personnel
and currency converter

bidders must register and receive their individual paddle numbers. As previously stated, if they are established clients, they will merely receive their paddle for the day. If new clients arrive, they will be asked for two forms of identification and to fill out a short form with name, address, and telephone number, and they, too, will then be given their paddle. Each registration desk enters the client's name onto the computer so that the Accounts Department is ready to process successful bids immediately following the purchase of any lot. The registration desks are usually open some fifteen minutes prior to the sale and can process a large number of clients in a minimal amount of time. These desks remain open during the sale, should anyone wish to arrive after its start and bid on a lot or lots well into the catalogue.

Bid Spotters

Sales in New York have traditionally been assisted by bid spotters. This practice originated on account of the shape of the auction room, where it was difficult for the auctioneer to see all the bidders. Columns still render this necessary. In a large sale with many people present, it is sometimes difficult for even the most observant auctioneer to see every new bidder. The bid spotter, sometimes behind a small podium and usually placed at the opposite side of the room from the auctioneer, toward the back of the room, or immediately beside the auctioneer, will execute bids on behalf of the actual bidder, raising the bid by the usual increment. Many experienced bidders like to work with a particular spotter, ensuring anonymity by arranging some discreet signal before the beginning of the sale. These bid spotters, who have traditionally come from the union crew, take great pride in their role and add much to the atmosphere of a sale. In some cases, once the bid spotter has identified a particular bidder, the auctioneer will take the bids directly. On other occasions, a spotter may have two bidders in his or her area and will be virtually conducting his or her own auction until one of the bidders drops out. Skilled auctioneers have good rapport with the bid spotters and retain some control at all times. New auctioneers are on occasion given a little gentle hazing by these auction-room veterans.

Bids Department, Telephone Bidders, and Client Service Representatives

Seated at long desks, often on three sides of the room, will be a number of auction-house representatives executing various forms of bid. They may be on the telephone directly with an absentee bidder, keeping the bidder apprised of the lot number being offered and ready to bid on the absent client's behalf. They may be executing written bids from the previously submitted bid forms. They may also be on the telephone with an important bidder located in one of the observation rooms, or "fish tanks," overlooking the salesroom. These are the people who sort out the complicated "either / or" bids, and they need to be skilled at ensuring that their client's high bid is effective by being on what is called the "right foot." Thus, if the client's high bid is $5,000, they need to be sure that they are not caught bidding $4,750, which would be the normal previous bid. There are several tricks that can be used to achieve this desirable result, including the point of entry into the bidding on an odd or even number, cutting the bidding in order to change the auctioneer's increments, or jumping the bidding in order to land on one's high bid. Since the auctioneer is also trying to avoid getting caught on the wrong foot as far as the reserve is concerned, interesting situations may arise. In the final analysis, the auctioneer prevails. Thus, a skilled bidding representative will either get on the right foot early in the game, secure discretion from the bidder to go "one bid over" the high-bid limit, or take the risk of executing that one extra bid. Most customers would be only too pleased to ensure the successful purchase of the item by means of the extra bid. With the vast increase in telephone bidding, there can be as many as twenty client representatives working the phones during a major sale, creating an essential element in the auction's success.

Departmental Specialists and Representatives

Seated or standing either on the stage or immediately in front of it may be a number of representatives from the department or area responsible for the sale. They may well bid on behalf of clients who prefer to work directly with a close associate from the department. Also among these representatives may be specialists from the same field but from another office. Thus, a London old-master specialist might be present at a New York sale of old-master paintings, bidding on behalf of a private client from England who may not even know the head of the New York department and has no former relationships with client service representatives in New York. These international specialists will usually be on the telephone with their clients, ensuring that they are as informed on the progress of the sale as possible. How does one know that these specialists are not bidding for themselves when they see an item selling for less than is considered a fair price? Employees of the auction house are not permitted to bid on their own behalf in a sale; this matter is treated with complete seriousness since the reputation of the auction house is at stake. In order to bid on an item in a sale, employees have to place a written bid prior to the sale and have to sign a statement that they have no knowledge of the reserve price of the item. They are, thus, placed on an equal footing with any other bidder except that they are not permitted to adjust their bidding as the sale proceeds. On the same issue, auctioneers are not permitted to bring the gavel down on their own behalf, should they see a bargain arising, since their knowledge far exceeds that of the bidder in the room.

The Specialist in Charge of the Sale

Immediately next to the auctioneer's rostrum will stand one or more specialists who were responsible for putting the sale together. They know every lot and the circumstances under which each is being offered. They also may have some telephone bids to execute, but their principal role is to be there to advise the auctioneer as the sale progresses. The auctioneer may consult with them at any time, turning off the microphone system and asking them any questions that may arise over the conduct of the sale. If there is a "global reserve" operating, in which overage above the reserve from a successful lot is applied to a subsequent lot up to a prearranged limit, the specialists in charge may be making these calculations as the sale proceeds and telling the auctioneer how much leeway he or she has on a particular lot. These specialists will also remind the auctioneer of any immediate salesroom announcements that have to be made. They are also useful in identifying bidders and underbidders. After all, they are likely to know the "players" in the room better than the auctioneer. In some cases, the auctioneer is also the specialist in charge, though the practice in New York tends toward auctioneers who, while they may be specialists in a particular field, sell in a variety of areas. A certain amount of knowledge in the field in which one is selling is useful, but practice has shown that a good auctioneer can sell in any area. The presence of the specialist right next to the auctioneer guarantees that all bases are covered and certainly gives the auctioneer added confidence that any situation can be handled.

The Auctioneer

The sale could not take place without this highly skilled practitioner. The question has often been asked, "Are auctioneers born or bred?" I believe the answer to this question is "Yes!" There has to be a natural desire to be an auctioneer. To be any good, the auctioneer, as the actor, must want to be on stage, at the center of the action, controlling all that happens. This skill is not, then, for the shy or the hesitant. A strong voice is an asset but not an essential in these days of electronic magnification. There is a need to be able to think extremely rapidly, while giving a sense of calm control. One may have to suppress one's emotions and expressions so that one does not convey to the room any sense of disappointment when items do not sell since this can have a dampening effect on the remainder of the sale. Conversely, an auctioneer must curb dramatic signs of triumph when a significant price level has been achieved; the successful buyer should feel that he or she has secured a good buy at an appropriate price and has not just been taken for a ride. The auctioneer legally and figuratively maintains control of the room. Thus, the need for dignity, stature, and a charismatic presence. I would also argue that a sense of humor is an enormous help to an auctioneer. If a session contains 300 lots of less-than-major distinction, the ability to entertain the room a little as the process grinds on has much to be said for it, although the auctioneer must remember never to entertain at the expense of the item being offered. The auctioneer must ever remember that he or she is representing the seller as well as the buyer in the vital moment in which a fair price is being established. Neither party should be at risk because the auctioneer imagines him- or herself to be an emerging stand-up comedian.

How is the auctioneer trained? My own experience is not atypical. For many years, I attended sales as an expert in old-master paintings. I knew all the ins and outs of successful auctions, fixing the estimates at the right level, establishing reasonable reserves, getting to know the regular buyers, watching the action in the salesroom year after year. Eventually, as I stood beside the auctioneer for yet another sale, I said to myself, "I bet I could do that, and besides, he's having all the fun." For the next few months, I would stand there beside the auctioneer, much more carefully observing where the bidding started, how the increments flowed, and how the auctioneer executed the reserves against the bidding in the room. I began to acquire a sense of the practical considerations that go behind the auctioneer's apparent ease of transaction. I then talked to colleagues about my desire to try my hand at selling. In the old days, there was less of a formal auctioneer's school. One night, I went up to our old subsidiary gallery, PB 84, and practiced for about an hour with an old auctioneer's catalogue. The next day, before I lost my nerve, I was to sell 100 lots of the most mundane property available, with a highest individual estimate of less than $2,000. This lowly beginning suited me just fine. A seasoned auctioneer started the sale and, after 100 lots, announced, "Ladies and gentlemen, there will now be a slight pause while I hand over the gavel to Mr. Hildesley." It is then that one's life passes before one's eyes. My throat felt dry. I was convinced that I would not remember any of my instructions, and that no one would bid when I offered my first lot. Of course, the people in the salesroom did not know that this was my first attempt. To them, I was just another of the young men from Sotheby's, in my case with a pronounced English accent that seemed oddly out of place at PB 84. The first 4 or 5 lots felt as if they took an hour to sell. Would this torment never end? And then, as I resumed breathing and noticed that I had managed to sell every lot so far, I began to get a feel for the rhythm of selling, found some strength in my voice, and, by the time I had sold 20 lots, started to think of myself as less of a fraud and more in control of what was happening. I began to enjoy myself, realizing that all those years had prepared me for this. Much of the auctioneer's training is osmotic. It was there in my bones. All I needed was experience and practice. To this day, I get nervous before a sale, like an athlete before a game. I believe this nervousness is essential to get the adrenalin running and to put the auctioneer at the top of his or her form. But the anxiety is one that is accompanied by the thrill of the anticipation of returning to the box and giving one's all. For one who works at an auction house, there can be no greater excitement.

Nowadays, training has become more systematic and formal. Would-be auctioneers attend "auctioneers' school" in which they practice under mock conditions. Seasoned auctioneers, fellow trainees, and representatives from the Bids Department create all sorts of situations as the trainee attempts to master the pace and the increments, while battling reserves, written bids, and unusual situations created to challenge their progress. This training will last for several months before the trainee is granted permission to apply for the necessary city license to conduct auctions, a prerequisite for conducting a sale in New York. (In my time, as now, the licence is issued by the Department of Consumer Affairs of the city. I lined up with a large group of folk who were applying for licences to operate hot-dog stands. One of my companions in this exercise asked me where my stand was. I responded that I operated at Madison Avenue and Seventy-seventh Streets. "How did you get that pitch?" was his astonished response.) Having secured a license, the new auctioneer still begins by taking 100 lots in a minor sale but does so these days with greater assurance that he or she has been appropriately trained to succeed. At the end of my first session, the auctioneer that followed me told the assembly that I had just conducted my first sale as an auctioneer, a practice that is maintained. The indulgent clients present usually encourage the neophyte with brief applause. One gets to know how an actor must feel on opening night.

The Sales Clerk

At the desk that abuts the rostrum or podium, the sales clerk maintains the auction records as the sale progresses. In this technological age, this is now done on a computer, which not only gives immediate access of the results to the Accounts Department and others who need the information, but also keeps a running total and analysis of the sale as it progresses so that the auctioneer can know what the running total is against the estimate and what percentage of the sale is selling or not selling. Next to the sales clerk is a backup clerk, keeping a manual record of the prices and the paddle numbers of the successful buyers as well as the underbidders, in the event that there is a problem with the buyer of record. Should the computer crash—and this has happened—this second record becomes the official record of the sale. The clerks are all trained to be able to record the sale manually. In a major sale, the auctioneer will note the paddle number of the underbidder as well. The clerks will also on occasion execute bids, doubling up their roles in order to make full use of all available staff.

This brief overview of the staff involved gives some idea of how complicated it is to bring each lot to its moment on stage. Behind the scenes are a large crew of unseen employees who make sure that the right item is lined up in the correct order to make its brief but vital appearance. The people that are evident in the salesroom are merely the tip of the iceberg, when you consider that there are over 800 employees in the New York office of Sotheby's alone.

The Setup

Equipment

The podium, rostrum, or box that houses the auctioneer follows the form devised in the eighteenth century. The canopy in the New York room serves as a sounding board, although electronic amplification renders this function obsolete. The podium raises the auctioneer slightly above the assembled clients, which not only gives the auctioneer a clear sight line to the room, but also instills a sense of control over the proceedings. The seat in the podium can be raised, like a misericord in a cathedral choir stall, should the auctioneer prefer to stand. This is a matter of personal preference for most auctioneers. It has been argued that auctioneers can exercise more energy when they are standing. I think that it is also a matter of height and body language. Shorter auctioneers may appear somewhat diminutive when seated. At 6 feet 5 inches, I personally have no option but to sit since, in standing, my head would touch the canopy. Some auctioneers vary their stance from sitting to standing and back again to add variety and freshness to their style. The podium has a microphone that is attached to the auctioneer and a switch that controls the light on the lectern and the microphone. There is also a small fan for hot weather, although the auction rooms are usually kept well air-conditioned to prevent buyers from becoming drowsy.

Above the stage are two screens. The one on the left in our illustration (see Figure 58) is a rear-projection slide screen on which may be projected slides of items too small to exhibit on the stage. Jewelry, for instance, is sold by this method. In the center is the currency converter board, which gives the bidders the currency equivalent in up to six currencies as the sale progresses. The Japanese bidder will know what is being bid in yen as the sale takes place, the board being controlled by a staff member operating a computer in one of the balcony observation rooms. When not in use for currency conversion, this board can also be used as a clock or the site of brief salesroom announcements. In repose, it tends to say "Welcome to Sotheby's."

The Revolving Stage

Presentation differs from house to house and from location to location. London sales are more understated than those in New York, where greater emphasis has always been placed on the actual production of a sale. Sotheby's in New York is the only auction room with observation rooms and with a mechanical revolving stage. This stage ensures a rapid flow of objects through the salesroom and certainly heightens the drama with which each lot is presented. I well remember the prototype of this mechanism when it made its first appearance at Madison Avenue. The mechanism wobbled horribly, leaving the audience aghast at the possibility of the porcelain on view falling off the moving easel. The porter on duty behind the stage attempted to rectify this anxiety by accompanying the next lot and holding it openly to assuage the audience's fears. Unfortunately, the porter involved, subject to the horrendous vibrations of the machine, wobbled just as violently as the porcelain vase he held, and the audience was reduced to nervous giggles as technology made its advances before their eyes. The current mechanism, efficient and smooth, became an unusual vehicle when, at John Marion's retirement party, it was used to introduce a surprise. Mystery guest and now honorary auctioneer, Bill Cosby, who hove into sight, seated on a Chippendale chair, greeted the astonished retiring auctioneer, and then proceeded to offer John Marion for sale, having previously arranged that no one would bid for him until John's lawyer, acting on behalf of his wife, Anne, offered a paltry $10 for the leading auctioneer of this century.

The Auction Itself

The Auctioneer

The auctioneer has mounted the podium. Pen in one hand, gavel in the other, the auctioneer's catalogue open on the lectern, he or she opens up the proceedings by making the legally required salesroom announcement as follows:

Good morning (or afternoon or evening) ladies and gentlemen, we offer for your competition today a sale of. . . .

I call to your attention the Conditions of Sale printed in the front of your catalogue. I draw particular attention to Article One which states that everything is sold under the Terms of Guarantee and on an "as is" basis. Further, Article Ten states that you are responsible for state and local taxes where applicable unless you are exempt from these taxes by law.

A buyer's premium is added to the hammer price of each lot

offered today and applicable sales tax is paid on the aggregate of the two figures. The buyer's premium is 15% of the successful bid price up to and including $50,000, and 10% on any amount in excess of $50,000.

The auctioneer may open bidding on any lot by placing a bid on behalf of the seller. The auctioneer may further bid on behalf of the seller, up to the amount of the reserve, by placing successive or consecutive bids for a lot, or by placing bids in response to other bidders.

The following lots have been withdrawn from the sale: . . . .

We begin this session with Lot. . . .

The Auctioneer's Catalogue

In front of the auctioneer is the auctioneer's catalogue, with the reserves marked in red. The auctioneer must not sell an item below this price. Next to the reserves are written bids on those lots that have received them, some of which will be below the reserve and others above it. Where there are two identical written bids, the first one received has priority and is listed above the second one received. The auctioneer glances at the reserve, then at the bids, compares them with the estimate, and, with great dispatch, he or she decides at which level to open the bidding, bearing in mind the need to wind up selling the item at the reserve if there is only one bidder in the room. In addition, the auctioneer is checking to make sure that there are no salesroom announcements on the particular lot. At the beginning of the sale, the bidding might begin at around half the low estimate, low enough to encourage potential bidders to enter the bidding, but not so low that it will take forever to reach the actual value.

Lot Order

Lots are offered in the order in which they appear in the catalogue. A few exceptions occur. A lot that cannot be found backstage would be skipped and returned to upon discovery. A lot that has been mistakenly bid upon would be brought back and reoffered, starting from the opening price, since on the first occasion the counterbid was false. A dispute over who was bidding could also engender a reoffering. If the wrong lot has been displayed on stage, the lot is sold over in order to ensure that there is no confusion as to who was bidding on what. When a lot has to be reoffered, this is done as soon as possible to make sure that as many of the original bidders are present as possible. Following the reoffering of a lot, the sale returns to the regular order. These events are rare, but the auctioneer must be ready to break the rhythm of a sale to make certain that a fair sale has been conducted.

Bidding Increments

The bidding increments are at the discretion of the auctioneer, but certain conventions are usually followed. The bids are taken in approximately 10 percent increments. Thus, if the bidding opens at $100, the next bid would be $110. At $200, the bidding either goes in increments of $20—$220, $240, $260, and so on—or, my preferred route, in increments of $25: $225, $250, $275, and so on. At $500, the increment becomes $50; at $1,000, it becomes $100; at $2,000, it becomes $250; and so forth up the scale. Thus, at $1 million, the increment becomes $100,000. Just as important as the amount of the increment is for auctioneers to remain consistent in whatever pattern they choose so that bidders and bid spotters know what is coming next. This also helps with the all-important rhythm or flow of the sale. These increments, which establish the pace of a sale, are not, however, sacrosanct. Skilled bidders or agents who have been set specific limits will on occasion "cut the bid" with a horizontal slice of the hand as a signal, indicating that where the increment might be $500, they are offering $250. The auctioneer is at liberty to accept or refuse such bids. Normal practice is to allow the first one since it may, indeed, be a bidding limit. Subsequent attempts may be refused as it becomes apparent that the bidder is attempting to lower the bidding pace and the price by reducing the increments. Aggressive bidders may also "jump the bid" by raising the bidding several increments at once. The sale is going along smoothly—$1,100, $1,200, $1,300 . . .—when the bidder suddenly says $2,000. This is designed to discourage the competition and is usually executed prior to reaching the actual value. I've yet to see an auctioneer refuse a jumped bid, but I doubt if professional bidders are much influenced by this show of bravado.

Sales Pace

I have already alluded to the rhythm and pace of a sale. The more important the sale, the slower it will go to some extent since the bidding tends to be more extensive and the likelihood of exceeding the presale estimates increases. In calculating when a particular lot will appear, a rate of one lot per minute is considered relatively slow, whereas two lots per minute is about as fast as an auctioneer can reasonably go while still giving each lot its fair chance. The lot-per-minute rate will vary according to the amount of interest displayed in a particular item. If there is no interest, an item will be bought in as little as half a minute. If there are many bids both in the room and on the telephone, a lot may take as much as five minutes. It helps when an auctioneer maintains a steady pace but varies it occasionally to prevent boredom in the room. To those not experienced in auctions, the pace seems fast.

Professional fine-arts auctioneers do not engage in endless noisy harangues like their counterparts at tobacco and horse sales. In fact, fine-arts auctioneers waste little time even describing the lot, recognizing that all the bidders have the catalogue before them and know what they are interested in and how much they are prepared to bid. The more quickly the item sells, the more efficient the process and the happier the clients will be. It is also true that the more items that can be sold in a session, the quicker the flow of property through the auction house and the greater the potential profit becomes. Visions of selling two lots a minute, twenty-four hours a day, around the clock, with a corps of marathon auctioneers are a little far-fetched; nevertheless, much of the money earned by major auction houses is made by moving vast quantities of works of art through the rooms as quickly and as accurately as possible.

Identifying the Bidder

A good auctioneer makes sure that everyone involved knows which bid is being accepted. This is achieved by identifying either the location or some distinguishing feature of the bidder, who should not be offended by being singled out. The practice assures that bidders do not stop bidding in the mistaken belief that it is their bid that the auctioneer has recognized. The auctioneer will say, "It's the lady's bid, on the left front aisle," or "It's the gentleman's bid, standing by the column," or "It's your's, madam, in the pink hat, in the second row." Such identification clarifies the process and removes any doubt as to whose bid is being recognized.

Bidding Signals

Much is made of the mystique of bidding signals—mainly on television and in film. Major buyers seeking anonymity do, indeed, use their own private signals. These must always be arranged prior to the sale with the auctioneer or bidding representative. They should be clear, precise, and not subject to misinterpretation. The placing and removing of eyeglasses, the holding of lapels, the raising and lowering of pens and other objects are all fairly frequent. One of the most sophisticated that I have observed is that of a dealer who arranged that he would be bidding on a certain lot as long as he was *not* in the salesroom. As his selected lot came up, he ostentatiously got up and walked out of the room, signaling to the relief of his competitors in the trade that he was not interested in this particular painting. The auctioneer bid against the room until he finally hammered it down to the unknown bidder. The dealer in question then reentered the room to be told by his fellow dealers that he had just missed a great picture. I will never forget his smile of satisfaction as he merely said, "Oh, really," and rejoined his colleagues for the following lots. Such a bid is now only legal if the auctioneer has been given a preset upper limit of bid. This can, of course, be way above the expected final price of the lot. Most auctioneers would, nevertheless, insist on a precise instruction.

Buyer Identification

When the hammer has finally come down on a lot, the auctioneer will need to identify the paddle number of the successful bidder. This is repeated to ensure that there is no confusion and to guarantee that the sales clerk is entering the correct number. As the sale progresses, a competent auctioneer will have either memorized or noted the most active paddle numbers so that the winning bidder does not have to wave his or her paddle continually in the air. Should the lot be sold to an order bidder either from the auctioneer's catalogue or through a customer service agent, the order number, which at Sotheby's is preceded by the letter "L" (which stands for "logical number"), will be ascertained and recorded in the auctioneer's catalogue along with the successful price. The auctioneer's catalogue remains the official record of the sale and is signed by the auctioneer at the end of each session. Major sales are also tape-recorded so that bidding can be reviewed in the event of a dispute.

Immediate Payment and Delivery

A buyer may walk less than 100 feet to the Accounts Department, pay for the item, proceed to the Shipping Department immediately next to the payment counter, and pick up his or her new purchase within minutes of having executed a successful bid. This immediate gratification comes courtesy of computerization. For that particular lot, the process is complete. As the purchaser leaves the building, a new potential seller is bringing in a work of art for a provisional presale estimate. The process continues, and, once again, the auction house gets ready to perform its function at the center of the art market.

A Glossary of Auctioneer's Terms

As with any professional body, auctioneers use certain terms whose meaning may not be immediately clear to the newcomer. Each auctioneer develops his or her own language and style. The following phrases are among those most often heard in this author's experience. Not every auctioneer will use any or all of them, and some will use phrases not covered. The uninitiated should not become intimidated by the jargon since the basic action of bidding remains extraordinarily simple.

"It's against you"

This means that the auctioneer has received a bid from another person, has a bid in the book, or is operating the seller's reserve against your bid. This phrase will only be used to identify a bidder who has already entered the bidding. If it's "against you," you no longer have the leading bid.

"It's against the room" or "The bid is here" or "On the phone"

Here, the auctioneer is making it clear that the bid being enunciated is either in his book or on the telephone. If it is in the book, it could be a reserve or an order bid. A telephone bidder will frequently be recognized in person to prevent confusion between multiple telephone bidders. Thus, "It's Tiffany's bid, on the phone," refers to a telephone bid being executed by Tiffany Dubin against the bidding in the salesroom.

"To the order" or "On / in the book" or "An absentee bidder"

This indicates that the auctioneer is executing a written bid. The auctioneer may not use this phrase to describe the action of protecting a lot with a reserve.

"I'm selling this at . . ."

This phrase may only be used if it is true. Therefore, when an auctioneer says this, the room is being told that the reserve has been met and a bid will secure the item. Since reserves are confidential, a good auctioneer will not make it obvious when this level has been reached. However, if an item is available to be sold at well below its estimate, it is sometimes worth letting potential bidders know of this possibility.

"With the hammer"

Sometimes a bid will be made just as the hammer is coming down. The auctioneer has the right to cancel the first "sale" and continue the bidding. Since this practice tends to annoy the first "successful bidder," auctioneers also retain the right to allow the first sale to stand, encouraging the second bidder to bid more quickly in the future. Repetitive use of this phrase means that the auctioneer is either not concentrating or has lost control of the bidders.

"Going once, going twice, sold" or ". . . gone"

This refrain, the pet of filmmakers and amateur auction-eers, is, in my opinion, misleading and superfluous. A gentle reminder that one is about to bring the gavel down such as "All through, then," or "Last chance, then," achieves the result less dramatically and makes the auc-tioneer look less foolish when and if the bidding picks up again and goes on for several more increments.

"Passed," or "Bought in" or "Unsold"

Any of these words will be used when the auctioneer brings the hammer down on an unsold lot. The laws of the state of New York require that unsold items be an-nounced as such. It is amusing to observe the style with which some auctioneers pass through this necessary state-ment, on occasion almost achieving a sense of satisfaction at this unwelcome turn of events. One is certainly not required to shout the offending word, and, while some auctioneers almost whisper it, seasoned bidders will know that an item hasn't sold merely by observing the pattern of the bidding and how long the auctioneer has been left hanging with the final bid.

V

The Auction House:
A Full-Service Resource to
the Art World

WHILE THE principal business of the major auction houses remains the selling of works of art at auction, they have long discovered that, in order to maintain a competitive edge, they must provide their clients with as many of their art-related needs as possible, in much the same way that full-service banks do everything they can for their clients that is permitted by the regulators. My experience springs from my connection to Sotheby's, and I will illustrate this section with examples from that organization. Christie's certainly provides the equivalent to many of these services, and other international and local auction rooms will provide some of these services. This will be most particularly true in the area of appraisals, which auction houses are uniquely qualified to provide since they operate at the center of the marketplace and, therefore, are completely up to date on current market value.

Appraisals, Fair Market Value, and Insurance

The art of making an accurate appraisal will come naturally to one who is used to putting together a sales catalogue. Every time an estimate is made, a form of appraisal is taking place. Needless to say, every estimate—and, thus, every appraisal—is but the expression of an opinion, and that opinion is only as good as the expertise of the one who forms it. The opinion of, or the value placed on, an object of art in an appraisal will vary according to the specific purpose of that appraisal. There is no one value that covers all contingencies. In seeking an appraisal, a client must make the purpose of the appraisal clear to the auction house.

In broad terms, there are three principal forms of appraisal: insurance, estate, and fair market value. In practice, the insurance appraisal is made at "replacement value," which is what it would cost to walk into a gallery and buy the identical item today. The IRS requires estate appraisals to be made at fair market value, and, thus, the estate appraisal and the fair-market-value appraisal demand the same level of value. Fair-market-value appraisals are made for a multitude of purposes, among them gift-tax requirements, family division, asset management, and estate-planning purposes. It is interesting to note that in reviewing submitted evaluations, the IRS Art Advisory Panel, composed of dealers, museum officials, and auction-house representatives, are not told whether the appraisal is for estate or gift-tax purposes, even though the unscrupulous taxpayer will attempt to make the estate-tax appraisal as low as possible and the gift-tax appraisal as high as possible. Taxpayers should bear in mind that the art world is relatively small, that at least some of the panel members are likely to recognize important works from major collections, and that the penalties for misappraisal far outweigh the advantages of "pushing the envelope."

The authorities have conveniently defined fair market value for us. It is "the price at which the property would change hands between a willing buyer and a willing seller, on the open market, neither being under compulsion to buy or sell and both parties having reasonable knowledge of relevant facts. . . ." I believe that it could be argued that the price obtained at auction comes close to meeting this definition since there had to have been a willing buyer and a willing seller, or no transaction would have taken place. The auction is an open, public market. The only compulsion involved might be the need to raise money, but most items sold in the international auction market do not sell under distress circumstances. Reasonable knowledge of relevant facts is provided by the scholarly and informative material contained within the catalogue. Even if it were argued that the auction market is not completely open and available to all (an argument that I would not accept), the issue becomes moot when it is realized that the authorities use the auction price records as their principal means of assessing the accuracy of submitted appraisals.

In seeking the services of an appraiser, whether from an auction house or a professional appraisal company, the collector is advised to observe certain precautions. Appraisal has become a highly specialized business. Gone are the days of the gifted generalist willing to enter one's home and appraise everything from the Remington bronze to the Remington shaver. The collector must ensure that the appraiser is qualified to render an appraisal in the particular field or fields involved. Sotheby's may use a team of up to a dozen different experts to appraise a multiple property. A number of years experience is desirable since the qualifications of the experts have to be annexed to the submitted appraisal. Appraisers should be prepared to list their qualifications and experience, and to give references of past satisfied clients. Any hesitation may be an indication that the collector should proceed elsewhere.

Collectors should expect to pay a reasonable fee for appraisal services. There are two main ways of charging for these services. The appraiser may charge a percentage

of the value appraised. This method of charging is justi-
fied by the principle that the higher the value, the greater
the responsibility of the appraiser in being prepared to
support the appraisal throughout the government review
system. In a major case, this could go all the way to the
Supreme Court in a lengthy, time-consuming, and expensive process. Behind this method lurks the specter of the
appraiser valuing the items more highly in order to
achieve a greater fee. This criticism can be laid to rest if
the appraiser offers the client the alternative of the percentage or the second-fee method, whichever is the lesser,
with a minimum charge. The second-fee method is based
on the number of experts involved and the time spent at a
per diem rate. The more senior experts charge at a higher
rate, just as partners in a law firm are more expensive on
the clock than associates. The vital thing is to agree on the
fee basis and any maximum or minimum costs before the
appraisal inspection is made. The major houses are glad
to provide fee estimates, usually after a site visit, in order
to avoid confusion and upset at a later date.

Prior to the preparation of the appraisal, the auction
house or appraiser is likely to require the signing of an
appraisal agreement, which not only signifies the purpose
of the appraisal, but also states the limitations by which
the appraiser wishes to be bound as well as the agreed-
upon fee structure. The sample on pages 195–197 is a copy
of a typical appraisal agreement from Sotheby's.

APPRAISAL AGREEMENT FORM

Appraisal Agreement

August 24, 1995

Name
Address

Dear (NAME):

This letter agreement (the "Agreement") will confirm your request that Sotheby's furnish you with a written appraisal of the [fair market or insurance] value of the items of property described [in schedule A to be attached hereto] OR [as   ] and located at [   ] (collectively, the "Property").

It is agreed that the appraisal, including without limitation, all copies, summaries and drafts thereof (collectively, the "Appraisal"):

(i) represents our best judgment and opinion as to the current [fair market or insurance] value and any other matters covered therein, and is not a statement or representation of fact;

(ii) is not to be deemed a representation or warranty with respect to the authenticity of authorship, period of creation, description, genuineness, attribution, provenance, title or condition of the Property and to the extent that any item of Property is appraised from a photograph, it is presumed in providing a value that the item is in good condition;

(iii) is not to be deemed a representation or warranty that the Property will bring the appraised value if offered for sale at public auction or otherwise;

(iv) except as is stated in (v) below, is not furnished and will not be used or relied upon, by you or any third party in connection with any transaction involving the Property, including but not limited to any purchase, sale, loan, donation or exchange; and

(v) is requested by the undersigned solely for [estate tax or family division] or [insurance] purposes.

In consideration of our furnishing the Appraisal, you hereby release Sotheby's, Inc., its parent, subsidiaries and affiliated entities and the officers, directors, employees and agents of each of them (collectively, "Sotheby's") from any liability or damages whatsoever arising out of or related to the Appraisal or the Property and agree to indemnify and hold Sotheby's harmless from any claims, actions, liabilities, damages or expenses (including reasonable attorney's fees) incurred as a result of claims based on or related to the Appraisal or the Property. You further agree that Sotheby's will not be required by subpoena or otherwise to appear in any legal proceeding, including deposition, relating to the Appraisal and that you will not at any given time commence any action, assert any claim or make any demand of Sotheby's in connection with the Property or Appraisal.

You represent and warrant that you own the Property free and clear of any claims, liens, encumbrances or interests of others. You agree that Sotheby's may consult others in connection with its Appraisal. Your representations, warranties and indemnity shall survive completion of the transactions contemplated herein.

If a blockage discount should be considered, you must advise Sotheby's by initialing the box below:

[ ] Blockage Discount

Unless you initial the box above, you understand that Sotheby's will not consider the applicability of a blockage discount and you expressly waive any claims against Sotheby's in relation thereto.

Upon receipt of the Appraisal, you agree to pay Sotheby's a fee of ____.

If you consign any of the Property to Sotheby's within one year from the date of the Appraisal, Sotheby's will refund at the time of settlement of the sale of the consigned property, a pro rated portion of the appraisal fee based on the appraised value of the consigned property. For example, if the Property is appraised at $100,000, and items appraised at $50,000 are consigned, one-half of the appraisal fee (excluding out-of-pocket expenses) will be credited to the selling commission.

[This Agreement may be executed in two or more counterparts, each of which shall be deemed an original, but all of which together shall constitute one and the same instrument.]

This Agreement will be governed by and construed and enforced in accordance with the laws of the State of New York.

In the event of a dispute hereunder, you agree to submit to the exclusive jurisdiction of the state and federal courts in the State of New York. This Agreement shall be binding upon your heirs, executors, beneficiaries, successors and assigns, but you may not assign this Agreement without our prior written consent.

Please confirm your agreement with the foregoing, by signing and dating this letter.

Very truly yours,

By: _____

ACCEPTED AND AGREED:

_____
[Name]

_____
Date

Because the appraisal business has no official licensing system, membership in professional organizations may help determine an appraiser's qualifications. However, potential clients should be advised that belonging to a professional body does not necessarily indicate that the member intends to subscribe to the particular code of ethics published by that organization, nor does it guarantee an advanced amount of knowledge in a particular area. In America, the principal appraisal organizations are the Appraisers Association of America (AAA) and the American Society of Appraisers (ASA). The latter group requires an examination for qualification as a senior member, but the standards of knowledge required for the examination are far from rigorous. The writer remembers when an expert in American furniture at Sotheby's was given the examination in European paintings as a result of a clerical error. Not wishing to waste his journey, he settled in, completed the paintings examination, and passed it with no difficulty. The Appraisers Association requires proposal and seconding by two existing members, followed by payment of dues. It can be seen that membership in these bodies is not an unconditional guarantee of quality in appraising, but at least the associations proclaim minimal standards and contain members who feel some responsibility for their professional status. The associations can certainly make a list of recommended appraisers in a given area from which the client may make a careful selection. The reputable auction houses not only contain a wide choice of qualified appraisers, they are also more than willing to recommend appraisers in fields in which the houses themselves have no specialist.

Having selected the appraiser, the collector should be aware of the minimum requirements for an appraisal document and description. The appraisal must contain the qualifications of the firm and the individual conducting the appraisal, and descriptions that clearly identify each object valued. In normal practice, appraisal descriptions do not have to be as elaborate as those of a sales catalogue. Provenance, literature, and exhibition history need only be supplied in the case of those major works that will be reviewed by the Art Advisory Panel, whose minimum value for review is $20,000. In the interests of practicability, appraisal descriptions will contain an item number, a brief description, notation of any signatures or distinguishing marks, measurements, weight where applicable, and date and country of origin when appropriate. This description should be followed by an individual value since group values are of little use in the event of a claim. Each description should be sufficiently detailed so that the item described could not possibly be confused with another. As long as this objective is achieved, unnecessary verbiage and proliferating adjectives should be avoided. In the case of many appraisals, a listing by room is desirable, the appraiser starting to the left of the entrance and proceeding clockwise. In multiple and specialized collections, while the room should still be noted, it is often more appropriate to divide the appraisal by fine-arts category so that all the furniture is together, all the paintings are together, and so forth. Clients should specify the number of copies of the inventory and appraisal required at the outset. Multiple copies are easy to produce from the master list and are always useful. A copy of an inventory and appraisal should always be in the hands of a lawyer or other fiduciary and off the premises in which the collection resides.

We have discussed fair market value and how it is calculated. How, then, does the appraiser arrive at the less tangible replacement value since the prices that dealers charge at retail are not only unpublished, but are kept in strict confidentiality. In the case of "insurance value" or "replacement value," the appraiser seeks to determine what it would cost to replace a particular item with another as similar as possible. Given that many works of art are unique, this opinion is bound to contain a degree of subjectivity. Nevertheless, a qualified appraiser should be able to arrive at this hypothetical value without much difficulty. One way of looking at it is to suggest that replacement value is the price that one would pay if one walked into a knowledgeable dealer's gallery that day and purchased a similar item. True, this price includes the dealer's costs and markup, which also include any profit the dealer is making on the sale; but, for immediate replacement, it is necessary to pay these costs. The fair market value at auction will in normal circumstances be below the dealer's retail price, unless the item at auction is of such great quality and rarity that the auction produces a new level of price. It will not take a dealer long to adjust a price label upward following such a sale. At the highest level, auction price and retail become very similar.

What, for instance, would be the replacement value of Rembrandt's *Aristotle Contemplating the Bust of Homer,* sold to the Metropolitan Museum of Art in New York from the Erickson Collection sale at Parke-Bernet in New York in 1961 for $2.3 million (see Figure 59)? One can hardly walk

Figure 59. Rembrandt Harmenszoon van Rijn,
Aristotle Contemplating the Bust of Homer

into a gallery on Fifty-seventh Street and ask for another example. There are simply no similar paintings available on the market. However, a professional appraiser will take the highest price paid during the recent period for the finest example by an artist of similar importance and then make a qualitative judgment between the two works, not forgetting the relative importance of the different artists involved and the logical difference between an auction price and the dealer's retail price. In 1995, this exercise might involve looking at Aelbert Cuyp's seventeenth-century Dutch masterpiece *Orpheus Charming the Animals*, which fetched $6.5 million (see Figure 60), bear-

Figure 60. Aelbert Cuyp, *Orpheus Charming the Animals*

ing in mind the price for Leonardo's *Codex Leicester* sketchbook at $30 million and coming up with a comparison. In my opinion, Rembrandt is at least six times as important as Cuyp, and this universally known masterwork must be more valuable than a superb, but nonetheless academic, sketchbook. I would place a sale estimate of $40 million to $50 million on the Rembrandt and would value it for replacement purposes at $50 million. This, interestingly, places it on a rough par with Van Gogh's *Irises,* which makes sense within the context of the overall art market.

In considering replacement value, a collector should be

aware that while fine works of art will, over a period of time, tend to appreciate in value, standard furnishings will not. Thus, the replacement value of an overstuffed sofa is whatever was paid for it out of the showroom. The moment it is in use, it begins to lose its value, and the replacement value and fair market value become more and more distinct. In carrying out replacement appraisals, thought should be given to separating the fine arts from the furnishings so that each area will continue to receive appropriately different consideration. The temptation to overvalue for insurance purposes should be avoided. The theory is that, when it comes to settling with the insurance company, such high insurance values will lead to greater figures, should a loss occur. Experience does not support this theory. The practice of "puffing" values has the effect of raising insurance premiums. In the event of a loss, the insurance company will negotiate the settlement based on its own assessment of replacement value. The company has access to the same expertise that the collector has employed.

Auction houses have broad experience in all matters relating to fine-arts insurance. It is well worth seeking their counsel when such matters arise. There are also brokers who specialize in fine-arts insurance. The auction houses will be glad to make recommendations as to these highly qualified practitioners.

Estate Services

Since estates provide a significant proportion of the property sold by the auction houses, it makes sense that the major houses have departments especially designed to cater to this important constituency, whose needs tend to differ from the living consignor. Often, an appraisal will be involved. There is also need for a full inventory and careful inventory control. In addition, the auction houses, in dealing with an estate, will normally handle a multiple or "mixed" consignment, usually through a professional fiduciary, a bank, or a law firm acting as or on behalf of an executor. Auction houses spend considerable energy in developing departments that understand these particular needs and in creating ongoing relationships with bankers, lawyers, and trust officers so that they know where to turn when the need arises. There are specialist lawyers who make a career of working in the discrete area of art collecting as it relates to taxation and other legal ramifications. The auction houses can once more make recommendations, should a collector be in need of such services. The relevant department can be found under Trusts and Estate Services. The personnel in this area are highly knowledgeable in all facets of estate appraisal, dispersal, and sales. The executor would do well to be in touch with this department early in the estate process and, ideally, during the planning stages.

Educational Programs

The major auction rooms offer a wide variety of educational opportunities through which collectors can increase their in-depth knowledge in almost every field of the fine and decorative arts. Programs can vary from an individual lecture on a specialist subject to a fully accredited, year-long postgraduate course, with many offerings falling between these two extremes. Short programs have been given in such diverse areas as "Art Deco in Miami," "Contemporary Art in London," "One Hundred Years of Jewelry at Auction," "New England Collectors," and "Old-Master Paintings." Seminars have been given on "Pottery," "Rooms with a View," "Imperial Russia," "Designer Decorating," "Folk Art," and "Landscape." Lectures are regularly offered on all aspects of the fine and decorative arts, usually available to the public either free or at a nominal charge. One-day forums have been held in such areas as "New England Furniture," "Still-Life Painting," and "Western Artists." Travel programs have been organized in which experts have accompanied small groups to art centers and regional points of interest all over the world.

The "American Arts" course, run from New York, exemplifies the thoroughness with which such educational opportunities are designed. Limited to twenty-five students a year, the course offers an in-depth study of American art from academic, professional, and practical points of view. In nine months, students examine every aspect of expertise, mixing connoisseurship with the inner workings of the art market and gaining hands-on experience of an ever-shifting wealth of material as it passes through the auction house. Field trips to commercial galleries, museums, libraries, private collections, artists' studios, crafts workshops, and major regional centers broaden the students' grasp of the art market in its multiple manifestations. All aspects of American art from the seventeenth century to the current day are studied, with reference to the traditions from which the various styles arose. Those who finish this course receive a certificate acknowledging their successful completion of thirty-six credits from what is an accredited institutional member of the national Association of Schools of Art and Design. The graduates from this program have gone on to assume significant roles in the professional world of the American arts, bolstered by the practical elements of the course that include study of restoration, client management, business development, and marketing.

Such learning does not come cheap, and the auction rooms charge at a rate comparable to other advanced study institutions. Few, however, can match the study environment provided by these market-driven institutions.

For those with a yen to learn more about the European aspects of the market, similar courses are offered in London, where Sotheby's is affiliated with the University of Manchester, offering M.A. degrees in Fine and Decorative Arts as well as in Post-War and Contemporary Art. As in New York, there are many opportunities to take short courses in many different areas.

The role of the auction room as educational institution should not be overlooked, most especially by those who want to gain that practical knowledge that remains an essential part of true connoisseurship. The auction houses provide frequently updated leaflets describing these worthwhile opportunities and are glad to make these materials available upon request.

Restoration Services

Since 1980, Sotheby's has offered a specialist restoration service, covering many aspects of furniture and the decorative arts. In consultation with departmental experts, work is carried out using the traditional techniques, in regular consultation with the client, and keeping careful records of the details of all work performed. In the cabinet shop, veneers can be replaced and cabinets can be rebuilt, chairs tightened, frames realigned, missing carving re-created, gilding refinished. Mounts and locks can be restored or repaired, all in consideration of a return to original condition. Expert gilders carry out a range of tasks, from repairing a flaking gesso to completely regilding a mirror, a picture frame, or a chair; the gilders grind their own clays and make their own gesso, upon which is laid the finest 23 karat gold leaf. A department is dedicated to the technique of lacquer. Fine Chinese and Japanese lacquers, as well as European and Continental japan work, are created in this labor-intensive department. Here, a variety of painted finishes are restored, from the smallest papier-mâché tray to a complete coromandel screen, the work sometimes involving months of painstaking detail.

Polishing is treated as a separate and distinct task, in which a final patina is achieved and new surfaces are made to match their antique counterparts. Brasses and gilt metal mounts are returned to their manufacturer's intended condition.

For many, restoration and its affiliated crafts remain a mystery, but at Sotheby's Restoration we believe that an educated client becomes a better curator. Courses in many aspects of restoration are offered regularly, affording collectors an opportunity to gain the necessary skills to become involved personally with the responsible maintenance of their works of art. Appropriate care of pieces of art can only benefit the entire art market in the long run, working to preserve what has been handed down from previous generations.

Real Estate Services

Both major auction houses now offer extensive real estate services, Sotheby's having led the way since 1976 and Christie's following in 1995. The concept is not hard to grasp. Having for two centuries sold the contents of some of the most exclusive and desirable residences throughout the world, the auction houses realized two essential truths. The first was that the major collectors would be interested in suitable property in which to display their collections. The second was that the auction houses had traditionally acquired a significant proportion of their property for sale from estates. What better lead-in to the potential sale of fine real estate than offering estates a full-service concept of estate disposition. As a marketing brochure proclaims: "Responding to the fact that buyers and sellers of fine works of art, furniture and collectibles are often looking to market or purchase their own distinctive properties, Sotheby's founded Sotheby's International Realty in 1976. . . . Sotheby's realty and auction divisions frequently interact to provide comprehensive services to their shared client base—offering the singular ability to market a property and its contents, as well as coordinate the sale of primary and secondary residences."

Figure 61. Sotheby International Realty Corp.,
European castle

Thus, the auction houses will not only sell you every conceivable form of work of art, they will also sell you the boxes to put them in. In addition, the international network of the auction house provides immediate access to prominent and wealthy potential buyers in the market of the very best real estate, many clients having several residences in major international locations. With its own representative offices throughout the world, the use of the auction house's regional operations, and an elaborate and far-reaching network of 190 independent brokerage affiliates, Sotheby's real estate operation comprises over 500 office locations, using over 11,500 agents, stretching from Beverly Hills to Sydney, Australia, from Palm Beach to Hong Kong, with plenty of castles in Europe in between (see Figure 61). The offices in London and Paris coordinate affiliate activity in Britain, France, Germany, Spain, Portugal, Italy, Switzerland, Greece, Sweden, and Israel.

The attractive nature of both the real estate properties and the fine-arts consignments leads to a combined marketing approach in which each discipline enhances the other. Regular and enticing brochures can be obtained from the auction houses, and, in the case of Sotheby's, the computer has been brought to full use. Clients may walk into the headquarters of the auction room on York Avenue and, through what is called a "computerized property display system," can view the entire worldwide inventory of properties, in full color, right on a computer screen, together with location maps and other details. An original screen displays a map of the world. The clients touch the area of the world that they would like to view, and, entering the price range with which they would feel comfortable, the current listings in that range will appear on the screen. Comparisons with recent sales can also be made through this computerized program. It never hurts to dream.

Financial Services

In an attempt to meet every need of the collector and further enhance the concept of full service, Sotheby's offers financial services that include advances on property that has been consigned for sale and loans secured by art collections not intended for sale. Generally, the auction house will lend no more than 40 percent of the total of its low estimates on the property, though this condition is subject to exception. The auction house also states that the minimum loan for consignor advances is $50,000 and the minimum for secured loans is $1 million.

Advances against sales can be particularly useful in meeting the needs of an estate. They also afford the seller an opportunity to overcome the inherent challenge of having to wait several months between consignment and actual sale, when there is an immediate financial need, which may well have been the impetus for sale in the first place.

These services recognize both the intrinsic value of major works of art and the fact that, while such assets should be bankable, they only become so when qualified by the necessary expertise. The accuracy of a major auction house's estimates is witness to that expertise, which is itself supported by a day-to-day experience of market conditions. Thus, collectors, who would not hesitate to take a second mortgage on their real estate holdings, can apply the same principle to their fine-arts collections, creating a fluidity in their asset management that can prove most useful.

On-Site or Country-House Sales

In certain instances, a property is ideally suited for sale on location. The property may have a distinctive appeal to a particular area. Such was the case with the collection of Dr. Henry P. Deyerle, whose Americana collection concentrated on the Virginia region and the Shenandoah Valley. There was little logic in removing this important group from its native Virginia, risking a lack of interest in New York and losing the intense local loyalty for the native works in their own territory. There is no question that the place to sell an "Extremely Fine and Rare Leather Key Basket, Initialed J. R. McK., probably Richmond, Virginia, circa 1830" is as close to Richmond as possible (see Figure 62). By offering this item in Charlottesville in the context of the Deyerle sale, it achieved a remarkable $36,000 against a presale estimate of $5,000 to $7,000.

Further reasons for holding a sale on site are those of convenience and expense. Large properties of attractive items in which there are no extremely valuable individual works may well sell better on location, thereby obviating the costs of shipment, with all its attendant risks. On occasion also, the property may be so overwhelming in size that a sale on site becomes the only sane solution. Such was the case of the sale of the contents of the Margrave von Baden's Neues Schloss (see Figure 63), which was sold in over 6,000 lots made up of more than 25,000 ob-

Figure 62. Key basket, Richmond, Virginia

jects, for a total of $54.7 million, including the remarkable price of $1.04 million for the gueridon, or tea table, by Swedish cabinetmaker Georg Haupt (see Figure 64). This sale took 15 days to complete and was the subject of a seven-volume catalogue. Local loyalty becomes an important factor and increases the value of the property as well as the magic of owning works of art with an undisputed royal provenance.

The major auction houses are ideally equipped to put together such sales, placing a management team on site and flying in the relevant specialists to ensure that each item has received its due attention and has been correctly catalogued. Sales in these circumstances become great social gatherings, gaining from the informality of working away from the surroundings of the major auction centers. Auctioneers shed their jackets as the heat in the tent nears

Figure 63. Neues Schloss, Baden

100 degrees, and bidders chew on sandwiches as the auction proceeds. These modern descendants of the English country-house sale have retained much of the bucolic atmosphere of their ancestors. Modern technology has improved the efficiency of this form of sale enormously. The telephone and the computer have made these provincial events as accessible as an impressionist sale on York Avenue in Manhattan.

On-site sales require a certain mixture of criteria to succeed, and clients who believe that their property would

benefit from this treatment should be guided by the opinion of the auction house, which knows the dangers inherent in this form of sale. Hidden costs are often high and
need to be carefully considered along with a myriad of
practical considerations such as the availability of a suit-

Figure 64. Swedish gueridon from the Margrave von
Baden sale, Neues Schloss

able site to pitch a large tent and accommodations to house large numbers of potential bidders. When the mix is right, highly satisfactory results may be anticipated. The professional's judgment needs to receive full weight in this matter.

Charity Sales and Benefits

Auction sales have become a popular method of raising funds for charitable purposes. Often combined with a dinner and even, on occasion, a dinner-dance, these events can have the advantage of raising money while being entertaining. There are, however, some tried and true principles that organizers of such events should bear in mind. These principles spring from over twenty years of participating in every conceivable form of charity auction, in which were sold items ranging from a T-shirt signed by George Foreman and a painting by ex-Beatle Ringo Starr to a ton of horse manure, to be deposited in the front yard of the successful bidder.

In an ideal world, the live auction is the main event rather than a postdinner entertainment. Combining the auction with a meal has some serious disadvantages. First, many of those present do not even face the auctioneer. Second, they are too busy having a good time with each other to concentrate on the business of the auction itself. Third, too much alcoholic consumption, contrary to popular belief, hinders rather than helps the auction process. To have the assembled crowd seated auditorium style, facing the auctioneer, is ideal. After a carefully timed auction, the attendees can then enjoy their dinner uninterrupted.

The ideal length of a charity auction is one hour. Since charity-auction lots sell at approximately two minutes per lot, 30 lots is an appropriate length of sale. Most seasoned charity auctioneers are unwilling to sell more than 40 lots.

Any number beyond this leads to boredom and a law of rapidly diminishing returns. There is nothing wrong with an accompanying silent auction containing up to 300 lots, providing a substantial crowd is expected. As a broad guide, I would recommend 1 silent lot item per guest. Many people will not bid, but some will bid on multiple items. In the live auction, organizers should calculate that approximately 10 percent of those in attendance will be active bidders. Thus, 300 guests will provide 30 buyers.

It would be impossible to exaggerate the importance of engaging a professional auctioneer for a charity auction. The "gifted amateur" who has always fancied himself in this role is unlikely to know how to pace, how to encourage bidders, what increments to use, or how to push an item when the action is heating up. The training and concentration required to pull off a charity sale are extensive, and failure can be extremely expensive to the charity involved. If it is essential to honor someone by having that person participate as an honorary auctioneer, let him or her sell the first lot and just that lot, and make sure that this lot is attractive but not of great value. The professional can then take over, more or less ignoring the style and pace established with the first lot.

Charity sales require the registration of the bidders and the use of paddles or bidder numbers in order to ensure that successful bidders accept responsibility come the cold light of dawn. Guests should register name, address, and telephone number. Bidders will bid much more highly when they are offered the opportunity to pay by check and credit card.

Charity auctions, which often include various forms of services, require visual aids. When an actual object is being sold, it helps to display it. When not displayed, an attractive art board or slide should be used. Clothing is impossible to sell unless it is modeled. Jewelry and prints do not sell well under these conditions because buyers are not clear as to what they are bidding on. How do they

know that the diamonds are genuine? Are the prints original or reproductions? Furs are now considered politically
incorrect.

Organizers should never accept goods on consignment—as when a car dealer gives a new automobile to the
sale, takes back the cost price, and allows the charity to
retain any proceeds above that cost price. The car seldom
makes the price, the dealer gets an inordinate amount
of unearned publicity, and the buyers are left under an
incorrect impression concerning the conditions of the sale,
creating potential poor publicity for the charity involved.

In a charity sale, the conditions of sale should be clearly
stated in the front of the catalogue, especially those conditions relating to warranties and the "as is" condition. The
auction houses are glad to provide organizations with
sample catalogues outlining these conditions. Organizers
should also be aware that a successful charity auction de-
pends upon an extremely hardworking organizing committee. General experience shows that it takes a full year
to gather together a worthwhile group of items for such
an event, which, in most communities, is best not repeated
annually. Care must be taken to ensure that there are no
competing auctions at the same time and in the same com-
munity. Communities can easily tire of being asked to bid
too often.

I have already suggested that a professional auctioneer
is vital. So is a highly effective sound system. It cannot be
loud enough. At charity sales, the crowd simply will not
stop talking, and the auctioneer, however skilled, will
need technical assistance in being heard. If the sound system is insufficient, the risk of the auctioneer having to
shout and, over an hour, losing his or her voice is very
great. If the auctioneer cannot be heard, the whole process
grinds to an unsatisfactory halt. A professional sound system remains the best expenditure the committee can
make.

The major auction houses provide professional auctioneers to charities. These auctioneers will normally perform without fee in return for travel and entertainment expenses. Many requests are received, and, in Sotheby's case, a selection has to be made as to which charities will be supported in a given year. Certainly, the auction house is pleased to discuss potential benefit sales with interested parties and can usually offer useful advice in the earliest planning stages.

"So, what am I offered for this magnificent ton of horse manure?"

VI

The Collecting Experience

HAVING REVIEWED the auction process, it is worth addressing the phenomenon that makes the process necessary and provides it with its lifeblood. It is the passion for collecting that has, over the years, brought together major groups of works of art. Over the centuries, museums have acquired the fruits of this collecting urge. The great collectors of the past, from the Medici in the sixteenth century to the royal houses in the seventeenth and eighteenth centuries, from the wealthy merchant-industrialists of the nineteenth and early twentieth centuries—the Eastlakes, Fricks, Havemeyers, Mellons, and Kresses—to the modern supercollectors—the Norton Simons, the Wrightsmans, and, more recently, the Andy Warhols and the Lord Andrew Lloyd Webbers—have all at some stage in their lives decided that the gathering together of great works of art is a civilized, worthwhile pursuit and a good use of their substantial fortunes. The cynical might suggest that such patronage springs from a desire to be seen as being able to afford such magnificence, but I believe that this is not the usual motive. The standards exacted by the likes of Louis XIV reach far beyond the urge for conspicuous materialism. The great collections have tended to display a distinctive character or concentration, reflecting the individual taste of the man or woman in whose name the collection was formed. It is my profound belief that the great collectors of any age are driven by a passion to acquire that is based on a conscious ability to discern quality in the realm of art. This same passion remains an essential element in the experience of every serious collector.

Given this basic desire to acquire and to possess, which appears to be innate in the human race, it is not long before the individual collector, possibly conditioned by surroundings and upbringing, turns his or her attention to a particular field. I believe that it is important to distinguish among three different kinds of acquirer since each displays a stage in the development of what I would regard as a sophisticated participant in the art market. These three types of acquirers are accumulators, collectors, and connoisseurs.

Most of us start as unconscious accumulators, gathering possessions about us through various means. Furniture is passed down to us from a previous generation. We marry and accommodate a weird assortment of wedding presents. We travel and bring back souvenirs from our journeys. We surround ourselves with symbols of our daily activities, views that we have enjoyed, books that we have read, adult toys that have at one time amused us, and so on. Our living spaces reflect our lives, our lifestyles, and our very personalities. The vast majority of the population never graduates from the accumulator stage.

The second stage is that of the conscious collector. Here, a desire to acquire is channeled in a particular area of interest, which may or may not have artistic merit. One is tempted to suggest that the person who collects rare bottles may be more interested in the varieties of form than in the aesthetic merit of a particular example. The collector will usually create a goal. Our bottle collector may wish to acquire an example of every Coca-Cola bottle ever manufactured. The collector of Rembrandt etchings may wish to put together an example of every etching created by this master. That collector could then spend the rest of his or her collecting life seeking to acquire the finest examples of each print as such examples appear on the market. This collector would need to have at least $20 million available in order to fulfill such a goal, but it would be technically achievable.

This last example brings us, however, to the third and most sophisticated level of acquirer, that of the connoisseur. The distinction between the collector and the connoisseur is to be found in the fact that the connoisseur (for such is the meaning of the word in French) does his or her collecting with particular knowledge of the field involved. The connoisseur develops a conscious strategy for achieving a particular goal, and that strategy must necessarily include gaining enough knowledge to be able to conduct business in a particular field on an equal basis with professionals in that field. Thus, the connoisseur becomes an expert. Not only does this expertise help in acquiring works of the highest quality, it also results in the connoisseur's being included in the company of those with similar interests. Acceptance among the acknowledged experts leads to unending pleasure since every meeting becomes an opportunity for the exchange of information and further knowledge. Any who might doubt this should experience the dynamics of a major antiques show such as the Winter Antiques Show at the Armory in New York or the private view of a major upcoming auction at Sotheby's. For the connoisseur, collecting is not just part of one's life, it is one's life. In extreme cases, the career that made the acquisition of the collection possible takes second place, and the collection becomes the prime motivation. I have in lectures suggested that the connoisseur collects with PRIDE, having created that acronym to define the five principal elements in the construction of the connoisseur: Passion, Research, Investment, Dedication, and Expertise. Let me briefly expand on these elements.

I continue to believe that passion must be the driving force behind collecting. Collectors must understand the need to fall passionately in love with whatever it is that they collect and to train themselves to resist falling in love with any but the highest quality of work of art. The selection of the area of collecting, while it may be governed by all sorts of practical considerations such as room space and financial ability, must first and foremost be governed by the fact that this particular area is the one that "turns the collector on."

Research or scholarship is the second vital ingredient. The most important advice incipient collectors can receive is what *not* to buy. This decision will be greatly aided by gathering knowledge of the background of a particular field. It does not make a lot of sense to collect seventeenth-century Dutch painting without first learning about Holland in the seventeenth century. The more one knows about the customs and costumes of an era, the way of life and the social history, the better the chances that one will begin to recognize what constitutes quality in a seventeenth-century Dutch painting. One needs to begin to understand the world in which a work of art was created. To cite another example, a Riesener commode is better understood within the context of considerable knowledge about how the court of Louis XV operated at Versailles. In other words, connoisseurs read around the subject as well as on the subject. Such scholarship is best gained through constant dialogue with acknowledged experts, in the auction rooms, the museums, and the universities, and in the finest commercial galleries. True collectors recognize that the learning process is never complete.

In the past twenty years, much has been made of the subject of art as an investment. The auction houses can accept some of the responsibility for this attitude; their marketing at the very least insinuates that high-priced purchases will lead to substantial financial gains over the long haul. It is demonstrably true that the highest-quality works of art appreciate at a greater rate than the lesser-quality works, but, as with fine real estate, this should not come as a great surprise. By the time one takes into account the changing value of the dollar and the cost of living, not to mention the expense of maintaining a collection, the art market behaves in much the same way as any other market, up and down, with occasional great rewards to those who have happened to be in the right place at the right time and who have been able to acquire major works under favorable circumstances. But overall, involving oneself in the art market demands the investment of both time and money in order to achieve the most satisfactory results. Given the sophistication of the art market today and the extraordinary growth in communications, bargains are few and far between. Indeed, I believe that perhaps the best rule to apply when it comes to investment in the art market is to spend just a little more than you can afford for the very best that you can find, which will force you to spend some time considering a potential purchase and will usually make you reach beyond the quality that had previously satisfied you.

Dedication is required in order to maintain a focus in a collection. Unless extraordinary wealth is available, it is impossible to create a broad collection of the highest quality. Although one can have a variety of elements in a collection, the collector is urged to concentrate on those fields that have been selected, making sure that they are compatible. This is not to say that American nineteenth- and twentieth-century paintings do not fit well with eighteenth-century American furniture, porcelain, and silver. I have seen several stunning examples of such happy juxtapositions. And some collectors overcome this challenge by devoting different rooms or houses to different areas of collection. For most, I would still argue for the selection of a definite theme or themes. The consistency thus acquired will add to the reputation and possibly to the eventual value of the collected works. In sum, "eclectic" is a dirty world in the art world, synonymous with lacking in discernment. "Pick your field and stick with it" seems to be the sounder route to take. Should a collector grow tired of an area, the auction house would be the first to encourage the sale of the first collection and a departure into a fresh field of endeavor.

The final element in these five is that of expertise, a gathering together of the particular knowledge required to collect responsibly and with a degree of sophistication and reliability. In all that I have said, I hope to have made it apparent that there is no substitute for developing one's own expertise. If life is too short or too busy to engage in the lengthy process of gaining such expertise, the next best thing is to learn enough to recognize such expertise in others. Fellow collectors, reliable and well-established dealers, senior auction-house specialists, and academic art historians have all spent years reaching such a level of expertise. These experts are proud of their knowledge and are willing to share it, often free of charge. It is a foolish collector indeed that does not make use of this vast fount of knowledge. I would argue that it is at its most available in the major auction houses; as the auction house knows, you may begin as a student, but the chances are strong that you will end up as a client.

As the collector's knowledge and expertise increases, the desire to increase the quality of a collection emerges. Dedicated collectors see their collections as living organisms, constantly growing and ever open to culling and upgrading. Collectors who have never sold when a superior example appears will wind up with static and less-than-satisfactory collections. Collectors who are prepared to sell all when they have found the pearl of great price will eventually reap the greatest reward from their collections, for, ultimately, it is the finest quality that will yield the greatest satisfaction.

At the end of the day, collectors collect because they are passionate about it. To me, there is little doubt that the great reward in this pursuit is not a potential growth in value, though this may surely occur. It is, rather, the "psychic dividend," the daily pleasure of being the temporary steward of beautiful works of art, the best that the artist or craftsman could create, whose quality will outlast the twists and turns of fashion and whose possession signifies the highest achievement of a cultured and civilized dedication to truth expressed in beauty.

Index